THE INNER POWER OF SILENCE

A Universal Way of Meditation

Other Books by Mark Thurston

Paradox of Power

Discovering Your Soul's Purpose

Visions and Prophecies of a New Age

Experiments in Practical Spirituality

How to Interpret Your Dreams

Understand and Develop Your ESP

Experiments in A Search for God

Meditation and the Mind of Man (co-author)

The Inner Power of
SILENCE
A Universal Way of Meditation

by
Mark Thurston, Ph.D.

INNER VISION
Publishing Company
Box 1117, Seapines Station
Virginia Beach, Virginia 23451
(804) 671-1777

ACKNOWLEDGEMENT
The author thanks Dr. Richard Peterson for his editing of the
manuscript and for his invaluable contributions to compiling the
appendix on meditation research.

This book is published by
Inner Vision Publishing Co.
Box 1117, Virginia Beach, VA 23451

This book is printed in the United States of America.

First Printing -- March 1986
Second Printing -- April 1987
Third Printing -- March 1988

ISBN 0-917483-06-5

DEDICATION

This book is dedicated to the memory of Lama Anagarika Govinda. Born in the West, he chose the path of Tibetan Buddhism for his life.

Although I met and spoke with him only twice, his profound teachings and his humble spirit have influenced my meditation life more than anyone else I have known. As a universalist, he had a gift for showing how East and West can meet — in a way that brings out the best in both traditions.

Mark Thurston
March 1986

CONTENTS

INTRODUCTION.

PART ONE. PRACTICING MEDITATION

Chapter 1. Why Meditate? 7

Chapter 2. What Is Meditation? 14

Chapter 3. How to Meditate 26

Chapter 4. What to Expect During Meditation . . . 36

Chapter 5. How to Use Meditation
                for Guidance 40

PART TWO. UNDERSTANDING MEDITATION

Chapter 6. Who We Are 48

Chapter 7. What Role Meditation Plays
                in Who We Are 58

Chapter 8. What Happens in Our Bodies
                When We Meditate 74

Chapter 9. How East Meets West
                in Meditation Tradition 90

APPENDIX. WHAT SCIENCE SAYS
                ABOUT MEDITATION 95

LIST OF REFERENCES 103

INTRODUCTION

MEDITATION
FACTS AND FALLACIES

Introduction
Meditation Facts and Fallacies

Meditation is surely a paradox:

Although one of the simplest acts we can perform on our own behalf, meditation can affect us in ways unachievable by any other personal act, no matter how complex.

Although popular beliefs put the roots for meditation in such Eastern traditions as Hindu, Buddhist, and Taoist thought, the practice of meditation is also deeply rooted in the Western contemplative traditions of Christianity — a fact unknown to most of today's Christians.

Although meditation seems to be a process of suppressing awareness of the body and the mind, it can have profound effects on all three levels of our being — physical, mental, and spiritual.

The meditator cannot *make* something happen in meditation. Strained efforts to force a change in consciousness only block success. Paradoxically, it is self-surrender and "effortless effort" that allow an inner awakening in meditation.

Facts about meditation are readily confused with non-facts and fallacies, some of which have been generated over the years to dissuade the average person from learning and practicing meditation. Try your own hand at deciding what is fact and what is fallacy:

1. Fact or fallacy?   The longer the period of meditation, the better.

2. Fact or fallacy?   The meditator's purpose for meditating will influence the effects of the meditation.

3. Fact or fallacy?   A meditator must have a specific "mantra" to repeat during meditation.

4. Fact or fallacy?   The body's sex glands act as transformers of creative energy during meditation.

5. Fact or fallacy?   Meditation can slow down some aspects of the human aging process.

6. Fact or fallacy?   Meditation is only a specialized form of prayer.

7. Fact or fallacy?   Most experienced meditators encounter a brilliant white light during meditation.

If you recognized that only 2, 4 and 5 are facts, you have probably had experience with meditation or writings about meditation. The other statements are misconceptions and in this book you will learn a different way of looking at some of those topics. But no matter how experienced or inexperienced you are, you will find the information and suggestions in this book useful in enhancing your meditation practice and your understanding of its importance.

To help the reader progress from the practical to the philosophical, the book is divided into two sections. Part One is a description of the practice of meditation — the whys, whats and hows. It covers the basics and yet it presents an in-depth picture of topics ranging from focusing techniques to getting guidance through meditation.

Part Two provides details and the philosophical foundations of the practical steps summarized in Part One. This section addresses ancient questions like "What is our human nature?" and "What role does the body play in spiritual enlightenment?"

In addition, an Appendix provides an overview of what science knows about meditation. Although some studies are referred to in Parts One and Two, more examples of meditation research are presented in the Appendix. The scientific method is more typical of Western culture and thinking than it is of Eastern culture. Although we can draw important insights from the East, a strong case can be made that Westerners are best served by working within their own tradition and world-view.

A book as brief as this one can consider parallel ideas from only a few of the great spiritual traditions of humanity. The passages chosen here for quotation are selected because they illustrate the remarkable parallels and points of convergence which exist. A deeper study of each of these traditions would show the uniqueness and individual flavor of each tradition.

The principal resources for this book fall into six categories with one or two authors representing each category:

Chinese Taoism. *The Secret of the Golden Flower,* translated by Richard Wilhelm, with a commentary by Carl Jung, comes from an esoteric circle of Taoism in China. Transmitted orally for centuries, the first printing was in the 18th Century. Wilhelm attributes these teachings to the Religion of the Golden Elixir of Life and its founder, the Taoist adept Lu Yen, who lived in the 8th Century.

A second source, "Spiritual Guidance in Contemporary Taoism" by Erwin Rousselle, appears in *Papers from the Eranos Yearbooks. Volume 4: Spiritual Disciplines.* This paper examines Taoist initiation, meditation techniques, and the pathway of transformation.

Tibetan Buddhism. Buddhism has many branches, each with its own meditation approach, but the Tibetan system is especially rich in technique and theory. Two books by Lama Anagarika Govinda are sources for the fundamental concepts of the Tibetan mantric tradition: *Foundations of Tibetan Mysticism* and *Creative Meditation and Multi-Dimensional Consciousness.*

Christian Mysticism. One source is *Mysticism* by Evelyn Underhill, first published in 1910. This long study of nature and development of man's spiritual consciousness is one of the most comprehensive studies of Christian mysticism and the pathway to enlightenment.

A second source, "Contemplation in Christian Mysticism" by Friedrich Heiler, also appears in *Papers from the Eranos Yearbooks. Volume 4: Spiritual Disciplines.* It traces the Western heritage of meditation and mysticism, and emphasizes the importance of understanding that tradition rather than adopting Eastern meditation techniques.

Modern Scientific Studies. A number of resources were used here. One is the dated, but still highly useful and insightful *On the Psychology of Meditation* by Claudio Naranjo and Robert Ornstein. Part One of this book, by Naranjo, is a philosophical study of different approaches to meditation. Part Two, by Ornstein, focuses on the psychological and scientific aspects of meditation and the implications of altered states of consciousness.

In addition, research literature of the past 15 years has been reviewed to identify research studies dealing with ideas presented in this book.

Intuitively Derived Information. Two extensive philosophical systems are used as sources for this category. Each of them is the product of the unconscious mind of a psychically gifted individual offering discourses on spiritual subjects, transcribed and published by fellow workers.

The psychic readings of Edgar Cayce refer extensively to meditation and the nature of human existence. Cayce gave discourses on these and hundreds of other topics from a self-induced altered state of consciousness. His readings spanned a period of over forty years. For this paper, the transcripts of the original readings have been used as they appear in the library of the Association for Research and Enlightenment, Inc., in Virginia Beach, Virginia (the organization dedicated to the investigation and dissemination of this material).

Two works by the psychic Ray Stanford are also used. *The Spirit Unto the Churches* is a collection of discourses on the physiology of meditation and the nature of the spiritual centers. A support team which included more than one medical doctor worked with Stanford to formulate the questions for these readings. *Creation* is actually one long reading given on the philosophy of humanity's origins.

Depth Psychology. The collected works of the Swiss psychiatrist Carl Jung form the principal source for this area. Jung was a pioneer of transpersonal psychology who took great interest in both Tibetan and Taoist philosophies. Although committed to working within the Western tradition, he appreciated the deepest levels of the human psyche where humanity is one.

* * *

All parts of this book contribute to the theme of its title: **The Inner Power of Silence.** In a society preoccupied with power, we must remember what real power is. The violence of manipulation, intimidation, or injury is actually only a caricature of power. These distorted attempts at power — too frequently taught and glamorized today — are feeble efforts to compensate for impotence. For example, we often try to rule and coerce others in the name of power when we lack the inner wholeness to inspire and lead others.

The real power of the universe is Spirit. A power not of our own making, Spirit can flow through us as a power to heal and to transform us physically, mentally, and spiritually. Although that power can surely manifest in our outer, material life, it must touch us first as an inner resource. Only in personal silence is that possible — a silence that is not merely the absence of sound, but a profound quieting of individual agendas, worries, and fears so that something universal can be felt. Meditation is not the only way to silence, but it may be the best and most direct.

The sub-title of this book also makes a bold claim: **A Universal Way of Meditation.** Is it realistic to expect that a common set of themes and techniques could be identified from the countless meditation systems available for study? This book proposes that such a cross-cultural approach is possible. In spite of divergent terminologies used, in fact humanity is **one.** In other words, a careful examination of Eastern and Western sources reveals, despite certain differences, a common understanding about the nature of mind and body, and the roles they play in meditation.

If you are new to meditation, we hope this book will help you take the initial steps to integrate meditation into your life. If you are experienced in meditation, we hope you will find new depths of understanding about it and helpful new ideas for enhancing your meditation experience and its value to you.

PRACTICING MEDITATION

Chapter 1. Why Meditate?

Chapter 2. What Is Meditation?

Chapter 3. How to Meditate

Chapter 4. What to Expect During Meditation

Chapter 5. How to Use Meditation for Guidance

Chapter One
Why Meditate?

Do you ever feel that life must be more than your body, your belongings, and your physical experiences? Are you looking beyond the standard symbols of success — money, possessions, fame, influence — for something that can reach deep within you and spark an inner light? If so, adding meditation to your life may be the most important step you ever take.

Meditation is a safe, direct technique for reconnecting to our spiritual selves. Furthermore, when this discipline is carried out on a regular basis, we can realize a host of physical and mental benefits. For example, here are some results reported in prestigious publications:

- Meditation reduces stress and many forms of anxiety. Carrington et al, *Journal of Occupational Medicine,* 1980; Puryear, Cayce & Thurston, *Perceptual and Motor Skills,* 1976.

- Meditation can be an effective treatment for insomnia, hypertension, head- West, *Journal of Psychosomatic Research,* 1980; Charlesworth, *Psychoso-*

aches, and chronic pain.	*matic Medicine,* 1984; Kabat-Zinn, *General Hospital Psychiatry,* 1982.
• Meditation promotes creativity, especially in the visual arts.	Travis, *Journal of Creative Behavior,* 1980.
• Meditation just prior to studying or test taking may result in higher grades.	Fiebert & Mead, *Perceptual and Motor Skills,* 1981.
• Meditation may retard biological aging, especially in the areas of hearing, close vision, and blood pressure.	Wallace et al, *International Journal of Neuroscience,* 1982.
• Meditation practice correlates with positive marital adjustment.	Aron & Aron, *Psychological Reports,* 1982.

Of course, the beginning meditator should not expect these kinds of results immediately, although effects such as feelings of relaxation and stress reduction may be felt early in the regular practice of meditation.

Meditation traditions typically take a long-term view of the benefits of the practice. For example, a study of Zen meditation published in the *Journal of Clinical Psychology* (Compton & Becker, 1983) reports that the desired effects of Zen meditation — most notably, an increase in individual self-actualization — result only after about a year of meditating regularly. This extensive learning period is consistent with Zen philosophy and practice.

Considering the enormous positive potential of meditation on all three levels of body, mind, and spirit — especially on a long-term basis — we should not be surprised to learn that many thousands of Americans and others in the Western world have begun the regular practice of meditation in recent years.

The need for a spiritual ideal. The primary sources studied in the preparation of this book — both Eastern and Western in origin — stress the need for the meditator to consciously set a spiritual ideal for his or her life or, at least, to give considerable thought to the question, "Why am I going to practice meditation?" The Edgar Cayce readings provide perhaps the strongest statements concerning ideals, saying that "the most important experience" that a soul can have in the material world is to set a spiritual ideal (Reading 357-13). (These two-part numbers on the Edgar Cayce reading quotations represent the sequence in which the Cayce readings are filed in the library and archives of the Association for Research and Enlightenment, Inc., Virginia Beach, Virginia.) The word "ideal" is distinguished from the word "goal" in that an ideal refers to the "how" and the "why" of a course of action (i.e., the *spirit* in which it is done). Goal-oriented thinking is, instead, concerned with the "what" of an action or the results. The encouragement to consider ideals means to turn one's attention towards the *process* as opposed to the *product*.

Govinda refers to this process of acting from the basis of a spiritual ideal as a re-orientation — the "turning about in the deepest seat of consciousness" (1969, p. 124). This consists of letting one's life be directed by the inner, spiritual nature, instead of by the promptings of the outer, material world. While most seekers would agree that this inner-directed state would be desirable to attain, not all are willing to admit that one should consciously set an ideal for oneself as a step along the way towards this attainment. Some prefer to believe that, left to its own devices, the unconscious will eventually issue forth an integrated and enlightened personality — that the conscious mind has the responsibility only of getting out of the way and letting things flow. Govinda would disagree strongly with this attitude:

> Just as an artist will hold before himself the greatest masters as worthy examples, irrespective of whether he will be able to reach their perfection or not, thus, whosoever wants to progress spiritually, must turn towards the highest ideal within the range of his understanding. This will urge him to ever higher achieve-

ments. For nobody can say from the beginning, where the limits of one's capacities are — in fact, it is more probable that it is the intensity of our striving that determines these limits. He who strives for the highest, will partake of the highest forces, and thereby he himself will move his limits into the infinite: he will realize the infinite in the finite, making the finite the vessel of infinity, the temporal the vehicle of the timeless. (Govinda, 1969, pp. 44-46)

The need for purpose. What then is the *purpose* for meditation? Many of the sources warn against meditating to obtain something directly for ourselves (e.g., psychic ability or better health). Govinda even states that rebirth in the heavenly realms is not an aim worth striving for (1969, p. 239). Certainly these things may come as by-products of meditation and should be accepted and integrated into our lives. However, the real purpose for meditation should be to attune ourselves to the infinite nature of being — to allow the infinite to express in the finite. One who meditates simply to escape from this involvement with the material world and with other people fails to achieve the ultimate potential of the meditative process:

. . . for he who strives for his own salvation, or merely with a view of getting rid of suffering in the shortest possible way, without regard for his fellow-beings, has already deprived himself of the most essential means for the realization of his aim. (Govinda, 1969, p. 279)

Most simply put, the language of meditation is the language of love. And love always speaks of giving and self-surrender, instead of getting and expectations. The best purpose for meditation — in fact, the best technique — is to enter with a sense of *giving* of oneself, rather than coming to get something.

This is a very subtle matter, because sometimes our wantings and expectations are for nice-sounding things. But the most profound experiences of meditation are probably reserved for those times when expectations are shed for personal reward or benefit. In its place is the feeling of having given of self.

When you want to evaluate the *quality* of your meditation, try the following method: Don't ask "What did I get?"
That is not the language of love, even when you may have
received remarkable things like greater energy, or a feeling
of being out of your body, or a psychic intuition. Instead,
do your evaluation by asking, "How deeply did I experience
giving myself to something higher than myself?"

Describing the Taoist approach, Rousselle points out
that, from a psychological standpoint, meditation should
have as its aim the creation of a new way of being. Meditation changes the way we see ourselves and the way we see
the world around us. However, it can do this only as we
experience the union of the infinite (and, up to now, unconscious) forces expressing in the finite, and not just talk
about it abstractly.

> . . . to open the way for new and meaningful shifts in
> our psychological components is one of the essential
> aims in meditation. It is of fundamental importance
> that man should actually experience — and not merely
> note intellectually — the opposite pole in himself, his
> unconscious and his vital force . . . (Rousselle, 1960,
> p. 95)

In describing the psychological factors of meditation,
Naranjo arrives at a similar conclusion: that the purpose
of meditation is to come to the awareness of a new way of
being and then to give expression to it in the physical
world:

> . . . meditation is concerned with the development of
> a *presence*, a modality of being, which may be expres-
> sed or developed in whatever situation the individual
> may be involved. (Naranjo & Ornstein, 1971, p. 8)

Stanford's readings contain considerable material concerning the relationship between purpose and spiritual
growth. Describing various emotional disturbances, his
readings rarely attribute the primary cause to a past experience or a physical, structural problem, but instead to the
lack of a direction of energy within the individual. The

direction of energy is determined by the conscious purpose we set for our lives. Without this, the energy system that makes up the body and mind cannot be redirected to allow the awakening of a new and fuller sense of ourselves:

At times, the tracing back in an individual of the experiences that have led them is helpful. But there are those who have become caught in the belief that some experience itself was the cause of an initial abnormal dispersion of energy from one of the centers, drawn off of the "energy reservoir" (as it might be called in a sense) of the gonad center. *It is not the event itself, but the lack of direction of energy.* It is helpful to clear up the event or its aberrative effect upon the mind, but in most cases this cannot be done without a retransferral of that emotional charge in another direction. It cannot just go off into space. Hence, we say, *purposefulness* is the key. (Stanford, 1977, p. 12)

Finally, those who have set a spiritual ideal and understand their purpose for meditating must have a sense of devotion if they are to succeed. Referring to the importance of such a frame of mind, Naranjo quotes the sutras of Patanjali which make the point quite simply: "[Samadhi] is closest to those who desire it intensely" (1971, p. 63). Rousselle includes this quality of devotion as one of the prerequisites for those who consider taking up the practice of meditation:

Meditation is no concern for curious persons wishing to perform psychological experiments, but only for men of integrity, still capable of devotion, veneration and profound feeling. (Rousselle 1960, p. 62)

* * *

We titled this chapter, "Why meditate?" We identified some of the benefits of meditation for body, mind, and spirit, and further scientific evidence on meditation is presented in the Appendix. But ultimately you must answer the question yourself — by determining the spiritual ideal for your life, perhaps by answering another question, "What is my purpose in practicing meditation?" Answering that question is easier when you know more about meditation, what it is, and what conditions are necessary for its practice. The next chapter aims at giving you that information.

Chapter 2
What Is Meditation

Meditation is a primary discipline in many religious traditions. Furthermore, some medical and psychological approaches for treating such symptoms as stress, anxiety, hypertension, and headache include a form of body-mind relaxation, self-hypnosis, or "centering," any of which may come to be identified as "meditation."

In this book, six conditions characterize the process of meditation as we work with it. These six elements are drawn from both Eastern and Western sources, and all are necessary in our definition of meditation.

The Six Conditions in Meditation

1. Meditation requires **focusing one's attention.** All forms of meditation have this trait in common. Sometimes referred to as "centering," it consists of two factors: concentrating one's energies, and finding the center — the point of integration — of one's being. Meditation is not letting one's mind wander and not allowing one's attention to dwell upon fantasies or phenomena that may arise from the unconscious:

What IS meditation?

It is not musing, not daydreaming . . . (Cayce Reading 281-41)

The circulation of the light is not only a circulation of the seed-blossom of the individual body, but it is even a circulation of the true, creative, formative energies. It is not a momentary fantasy, but the exhaustion of the cycle (soul-migrations) of all the aeons. (Wilhelm 1962, p. 32)

2. Meditation requires **letting go of thought patterns** that have been controlling us and that have led us to a limited concept of our own being. The above definition from *The Secret of the Golden Flower* refers to "the exhaustion of the cycle" in which the soul is drawn back time and again into the material world (reincarnation). These limiting thought patterns, these habitual response patterns, are what draw us back into the earth. Our karma can be thought of as the collection of our habits. In meditation, we shift our attention and sense of identification to a more holistic and unlimited concept of ourselves and away from the limited and fragmenting nature of our habitual responses. Naranjo describes this as:

. . . a very *precise* unfolding of experience to which the individual opens himself as he lays aside his habitual patterns of thinking and feeling and his superficial identity. (Naranjo & Ornstein, 1971, p. 26)

3. In the three-dimensional world, we experience ourselves as body, mind and spirit. In meditation, the activities of **body, mind, and spirit are brought into an attunement** or state of unity. This concept is stated clearly in the Cayce readings and by Rousselle:

What IS meditation?

It is not musing, not day dreaming; but as ye find your bodies made up of the physical, mental and spiritual, it is the attuning of the mental body and the physical body to its spiritual source. (Cayce Reading 281-41)

All three, first the stream of the breath, then the

stream of the seed, and finally, the stream of the spirit, must be regulated by meditation, which guides and unites the streams. (Rousselle, 1960, p. 71)

4. The preceding chapter emphasized that the real purpose for meditation should be **to allow the infinite to express in the finite.** This experience must be part of the definition of meditation. Underhill describes this as:

... the breaking down of the barrier between the surface-self and those deeper levels of personality where God is met and known "in our nothingness," and a mysterious fusion of divine and human life takes place. (Underhill, 1910, p. 304)

Since meditation must include all six elements an LSD experience, for example, cannot qualify as meditation, although it may indeed break down the barrier between the infinite and the finite. It does so without an attunement of the body, mind, and spirit, and without the individual's having let go of habitual response patterns.

5. Meditation works toward **making the enlightenment of consciousness a permanent state of being,** and is not simply a transitory experience, as with drugs. *The Secret of the Golden Flower* uses the phrase "making fast" to describe this meditative process:

Fixating contemplation as indispensable; it ensures the making fast of the enlightenment. (Wilhelm, 1962, p. 36)

6. Meditation is **an habitual process,** not something done just once or occasionally. Govinda compares human consciousness to a musical instrument that frequently requires tuning anew (1969, p. 107). One of the most significant promises in *The Secret of the Golden Flower* refers to the *daily* practice of meditation, for even 15 minutes, which can permit an individual to move beyond karmic patterns that would result in coming back into the earth a thousand more times:

Children, take heed! If for a day you do not practice meditation, this light streams out, who knows whither? If you only meditate for a quarter of an hour, by it you can do away with the ten thousand aeons and a thousand births. All methods end in quietness. This marvellous magic cannot be fathomed. (Wilhelm, 1962, p. 33)

Thus, frequency and regularity of meditation appear to be a higher priority than length of meditation period.

* * *

These six conditions, then, lead us to the following definition of meditation:

Meditation must be an habitual process in which the individual focuses attention and lets go of thought patterns, bringing body, mind, and spirit into attunement, thus allowing the infinite to express in the finite, all with the goal of the permanent enlightenment of consciousness.

This definition guides our selection or creation of a procedure for meditating. Whatever technique we use, it must help the individual focus attention and let go of thought patterns. In preparing to understand the universal meditation process described in the next chapter, we will first explore principles underlying the self-control needed for holding a focus and eliminating potential distractions. Without such understanding, the process may not be effective, or in the words of *The Secret of the Golden Flower*, the "secret charm" (the technique) will not work:

All changes of spiritual consciousness depend upon the heart. There is a secret charm, which although it works very accurately, is yet so fluid that it needs extreme intelligence and clarity, and the most complete absorption and tranquility. People without this highest degree of intelligence and understanding do not find the way to apply the charm; people without this utmost capacity for absorption and tranquillity cannot keep fast hold of it. (Wilhelm, 1962, p. 23)

(Here we should understand the word "intelligence" to mean "wisdom and sensitivity" — *not* intellectual capability.)

Holding a Focus — Overcoming Distractions

On the issue of holding a focus, schools of meditation differ widely on the kind of mental activity to be made a part of the procedure. Some approaches emphasize mental images (e.g., mandalas, pictures of the Master), while others teach that all imagery should be ignored. The primary sources for this book seem to agree that some form of mental activity is needed, at least in the initial stages of meditation. Images other than the chosen focal point are to be ignored or expelled.

Evelyn Underhill, for example, refers to the first stage of meditation as "recollection" and says it is the most difficult because it involves an act of will to go against the habits and impulses of the mind. An individual may spend years in this first stage:

All the scattered interests of the self have here to be collected; there must be a deliberate and unnatural act of attention, a deliberate expelling of all discordant images from the consciousness — a hard and ungrateful task. Since the transcendental faculties are still young and weak, the senses not wholly mortified, it needs a stern determination, a "willful choice," if we are to succeed in concentrating our attention upon the whispered messages from within, undistracted by the loud voices which besiege us from without. (Underhill, 1910, p. 313)

Rousselle defines three preparatory stages in which the meditator moves from the constant flow of thoughts and images ("monkeys at the foot of a tree") to a state of stillness and peace:

[1.] You now enter upon the first of the three preparatory stages of meditation. All thoughts are bound fast in imagination to the body's center (eros!) like monkeys at the foot of a tree. The bond between *logos* and *eros* paralyzes the "monkey" thoughts. Consciousness by an act of the imagination is shifted to the solar plexus, i.e., the unconscious. This fixation is called *ting* . . .

[2.] This produces a certain degree of relaxation, though there is still a faint striving to hold fast. This second preparatory stage of release or silence is called *ching*.

[3.] One now attains the third stage, in which there is no further effort or tension, the state of peaceful beatitude *(an)*.

Now at last the stage has been reached in which something can "happen" to you. What you now experience is the content of your meditation — but images and ideas must be expelled at once! (Rousselle, 1960, p. 87)

In *The Secret of the Golden Flower*, distracting images that may arise after reaching a state of stillness are referred to as the "fox-spirits" (Wilhelm, 1962, p. 46). The text warns that to pay attention to these, no matter how beautiful they may be, is to settle for far less than the potential rewards of proper meditation. Instead, one must return to the chosen point of focus.

Naranjo identifies several characteristics of these points of focus which he found in his study of various approaches: First is *centrality*, such as in the cross and the lotus. These images evoke the notion of a center around which action flows, as well as a radiation or emanation. A second characteristic is an expression of *giving* or of *self-emptying*, as symbolized in the cross or as verbalized in portions of the Lord's Prayer. Finally, many of these focal points demonstrate *lawfulness* or *order*, as typified in the geometric order of a Tibetan mandala or in the symbology of the seed syllables of a mantra.

Cayce and Govinda provide very similar recommendations concerning the choice of a focal point for attention during meditation. Cayce refers to *"affirmations"* or verbal expressions of the spiritual ideal that has been chosen. His affirmations are usually from one to four sentences in length. Govinda's teaching is from the mantric tradition. However, the words of the affirmation or the Sanskrit syllables of the *mantra* do not work through any "magic power" within them. They come alive and aid in the transformative process only as the meditator dwells upon and experiences their *meaning:*

Mantras are not "spells," as even prominent Western scholars repeat again and again, nor are those who have attained proficiency . . . in them "sorcerers" . . . Mantras do not act on account of their own "magic" nature, but only through the mind that experiences them. They do not possess any power of their own; they are only the means for concentrating already existing forces — just as a magnifying glass, though it does not contain any heat of its own, is able to concentrate the rays of the sun and to transform their mild warmth into incandescent heat.

This may appear as sorcery to the bushman, because he sees only the effect, without knowing the causes and their inner connections. Therefore those who confuse mantric knowledge with sorcery, are not very different in their point of view from the attitude of the bushman. And if there have been scholars who tried to discover the nature of mantras with the tools of philological knowledge, and came to the conclusion that they were "meaningless gibberish" because they had neither grammatical structure nor logical meaning, then we can only say that such a procedure was like pursuing butterflies with a sledge hammer. (Govinda, 1969, pp. 27-28)

Pronouncing the mantra correctly, as if the vibration of the sound had some special effect on the body, is not even important. Govinda points out that if the efficacy of Tibetan mantras depended upon the correct pronunciation, they would have all lost their usefulness "because they are not pronounced there according to the rules of Sanskrit but according to the phonetic laws of the Tibetan language" (Govinda, 1969, p. 27).

Cayce states that Jesus gave the Lord's Prayer to His followers to be used as a focus for meditation (Cayce Reading 281-29). Its various parts are meant to affect particular spiritual centers within the body. Describing the way in which this prayer should be used in meditation, one Cayce reading says, "As in feeling, as it were, the flow of the meanings of each portion of same throughout the body-physical" (Reading 281-29).

As the meditator says the words of the affirmation or the mantra, there is an inner response to its meaning. That awakening may be a feeling or a state of consciousness, but the meditator should focus attention upon that response. Most people find that in a very short time the mind will drift off and start thinking about something else. At this point, the affirmation or mantra should be repeated. On the other hand, one who *continually* repeats it is not taking time to be aware of what is being awakened from within during the meditation. Holding to the *form* of the words so tightly that one ignores the *spirit* behind them does not lead to deep meditation.

Heiler points out this necessity to go beyond the form when he describes using the image of Jesus as a focal point. In his study of St. Bernard, he notes that "just as for Origen, visual meditation on Jesus is a preliminary stage, leading up to the imageless contemplation of the Logos" (Heiler, 1960, p. 197).

Naranjo presents the Sufi meditation technique which employs a statement of the ideal as a focal point. Of particular importance is the reference to the way the affirmation (Zikr) causes an awakening in certain spiritual centers and other parts of the body. The Zikr is not just repeated over and over, but becomes a total experience for the meditator, as is evident from the instructions in the final paragraph below:

This double movement of affirming the transcendent unity of existence and denying the attachments of the ego to partial reflections of the One Truth is the content of one of the most widespread forms of dhikr: the repetition of the words of the Prophet Mahomet: "LA ILAHA ILLA'LLAH" (There is no god but God).

The following passage from *Najmeddin Daya*, a thirteenth-century Sufi classic, is most explicit on both the outer and inner aspects of the repetition:

Having prepared a room which is empty, dark, and clean, in which he will, for preference, burn some sweet-scented incense, let him sit there, cross-legged, facing the qibla (direction of Mekka). Laying his hands on his thighs, let him stir up his heart to wakefulness, keeping a guard on his eyes. Then with profound veneration he should say aloud: LA ILAHA ILLA'LLAH. The LA ILAHA should be fetched from the root of the navel, and the ILLA'LLAH drawn into the heart, so that the powerful effects of Zikr (dhikr) may make themselves felt in all the limbs and organs. But let him not raise his voice too loud. He should strive, as far as possible, to damp and lower it according to the words "Invoke thy Lord in thyself humbly and with compunction, without publicity of speech." . . .

After this fashion, then, he will utter the Zikr frequently and intently, thinking in his heart on the meaning of it and banishing of it every distraction. When he thinks of LA ILAHA, he should tell himself: I want nothing, seek nothing, love nothing ILLA'LLAH — but God. Thus, with LA ILAHA he denies and excludes all competing objects, and with ILLA'LLAH he affirms and posits the divine Majesty as his sole object loved, sought and aimed at. (Naranjo & Ornstein, 1971, p. 48)

Most people find that various internal and external distractions are formidable problems in meditation. One becomes aware of the discomfort of the chair or of an itch. Outside sounds pull at one's attention. Perhaps the best technique to deal with these distractions is to *use* them as they come into awareness, rather than to fight them. In the words of *The Secret of the Golden Flower:*

To become conscious of the distraction is the mechanism by which to do away with the distraction.

Indolence of which a man is conscious, and indolence of which he is unconscious, are a thousand miles apart. (Wilhelm, 1962, p. 42)

The meditator may, for example, use the distraction as a reminder to return to the ideal or the spirit of the affirmation. To illustrate: An individual is focusing on the words "May I be a channel of blessings to others" and hears a plane overhead. The meditator can take a few seconds to pray for the people in that plane, letting the prayer bring the consciousness back to the spirit behind these words from which attention has been distracted. Such a technique takes practice and a degree of ingenuity to work with the mental associations that accompany various internal or external distractions. This is reminiscent of the Tantric tradition of turning a weakness into a strength. As one becomes aware of attention drifting off, the important response is not to fight the mind. This leads only to a cycle of frustration contrary to the consciousness we seek to awaken in meditation.

Breathing Awareness

Along with focusing attention, *breathing* is an important issue to be considered in the practice of meditation. The relationship between consciousness and the breath has been noted by many sources. For example, our breathing patterns when we are startled or afraid are usually quite different from those in moments of tranquillity. The meditator can use this principle to advantage in attempting to experience an expanded state of awareness.

Yoga exercises teach several breathing disciplines that many meditators have reported to be helpful when used in moderation.

Thus breathing becomes a vehicle of spiritual experience, the mediator between body and mind. It is the first step towards the transformation of the body from the state of a more or less passively and unconsciously functioning physical organ into a vehicle or tool of a perfectly developed and enlightened mind, as demonstrated by the radiance and perfection of the Buddha's body. (Govinda, 1969, p. 151)

There are certain types of practice which are based on such universal principles that they can be applied to all normal human beings ... The practice of *ānāpānasati* is the most important of them, and this is why the Buddha recommended it as the best starting point for any kind of creative meditation *(bhāvanā)* ...

It is in this respect that *ānāpānasati* distinguishes itself from *prānayama* (which has been popularized by many yoga teachers in the West, who follow the usual Hindu tradition): it does not try to control *(yama)* the process of breathing, in the sense of trying to impose our will upon it — which would only assert our ego-sense or the power-aspect of our ego, instead of overcoming it — but it tries to make us fully aware of this vital process by identifying ourselves consciously with its rhythm and its profound implications.

Thus we experience the very nature of life by surrendering ourselves to its rhythm, instead of interfering with it, because it is the rhythm of the universe that breathes through us. Instead of thinking ourselves as the agents and originators of this movement ("*I* am breathing in; *I* am breathing out," etc.), we should rather feel "the universe breathes in me, streams through me, it is not *I* who is breathing, but the universe through me."

... the process of breathing, if fully understood and experienced in its profound significance, could teach us more than all the philosophies of the world. (Govinda, 1976, pp. 118-120)

The preceding discussion of the special issues of holding focus, overcoming distractions, and breathing in meditation could be discouraging to a would-be meditator. So one must be careful not to get trapped in the Western attitude towards techniques that amounts to a desire for short cuts to spiritual growth. Our culture has grown accustomed to quick changes, but the transformation of consciousness to a state of spiritual attunement is a slow process. We have discovered that we can manipulate nature with our machines, and we are tempted to try to manipulate the powerful forces that lie within the mind by techniques that promise quick results. Because of the Westerner's fundamental misunderstanding of the purpose of Eastern meditation practices, Rousselle gives the following warning: "Oriental meditations are in large part unsuited to the European. He should undertake them, if at all, only under the direction of an experienced master, like every Chinese" (1960, p. 62).

The two techniques that have been described previously — focusing on an affirmation or spiritual ideal, and breathing (when done in *moderation*) — should be safe for the Westerner. The Cayce readings imply that to overcome any fear one may have of meditation, one should understand that the ideal or purpose held in meditation determines what is awakened and provides the protection.

* * *

Now that we have defined the basic elements of meditation and explored the special issues of focusing and breathing, we are ready to work in the next chapter with a universal technique for meditating.

Chapter 3
How to Meditate

This chapter presents one elegantly simple and highly practical technique for meditation. Of the dozens of meditation systems that exist, this eleven-step approach has a universal quality, drawing as it does upon recurrent themes and techniques found in most of the sources used for this book. This parallelism will be demonstrated in Chapter 7.

Step 1. Set a spiritual ideal for your life. Every meditation period should begin by taking time to remember a sense of purpose that leads you to the practice of meditation. If you have not recently taken time to formulate carefully the ideals that you want to have guiding and directing your life, now is a good time to do so.

What is meant by the word "ideal"? As pointed out in Chapter 1, an ideal is not a "goal," which refers instead to the *product* of our actions. An ideal refers more to the *purpose* for an action, or the *spirit* in which it is done.

The question to ask yourself is this: "What spirit of living do I want directing every part of my life?" In other words, ask yourself what sense of meaning and purpose you want to strive for in the way you live your life? Admittedly, not every action, thought, or feeling will reflect that ideal, because in our humanness we often fall short. But each of us can aspire to a profound sense of meaning — a higher way of seeing life and others and self.

As you determine your spiritual ideal, be sure it comes from deep within yourself and not from the expectations of others. In other words, a spiritual ideal for your life must not have a quality of "ought" or "should." Throughout our lives, our parents, teachers, and other authority figures tell us what our purposes and aspirations in life ought to be. A true spiritual ideal needs to come more authentically from your own self.

How can this deeper, more genuine level be tapped? One way is to draw upon the peak spiritual moments you have already had in your life. Each of us has caught glimpses — however briefly — of a higher spiritual reality. Each of us has tasted a deeper, more profound sense of purposefulness to life than the perspective offered by conscious physical life.

What were the peak spiritual moments of your past? They may have been one or two special dreams in which you seemed to be touched by a higher reality, or a deep prayer or meditation experience. Your peak spiritual moments may even have been in waking life — a loving moment with someone, a day of heightened creativity, or a special time out in nature. Think back over your life and recall several such special times — moments to be deeply honored and remembered, even though the business of daily living causes us to forget or ignore the impact they had upon us.

To choose a spiritual ideal then, take several minutes to sit quietly and remember these peak spiritual moments. Try to relive them and let these memories shape your thinking and feeling so that, for a moment, you *become* the person you were in those special experiences. Once you are in touch with that different place within yourself, allow into your mind a word or phrase that describes that state of consciousness.

For one person, the spiritual ideal might be "loving freedom"; for another person, it might be "oneness with the Light"; and for still a third, simply "service." No matter what words you use, they should describe a place of consciousness within yourself that you have actually touched and tasted. A spiritual ideal must be something living for you — not merely a philosophical abstraction.

In setting a spiritual ideal this way, you may sense that even higher ideals are possible. In fact, one's spiritual ideal is, in effect, a statement which affirms, "This is the highest meaning and purpose of life that I *know* as reality, because I have personally been touched by it."

Once you have set a spiritual ideal for your life, begin each meditation period with a brief moment to remember that ideal and its connection to the meditation period. Meditation is a powerful technique for moving you more quickly in the direction of the ideal you hold.

Step 2. Set and maintain a consistent time of day for meditation, even if initially the length of each session is brief. It's the consistency that counts. That consistency should include the regularity of daily meditation, as well as the keeping of a particular time of day for the silence period.

Examine your life and the various kinds of demands you encounter in terms of time and energy. Taking these factors into account, at what time of day are you most likely to be able to still your mind and body, and keep your attention focused upon your spiritual ideal? That is the best time of day for you. For one person, it may be the first thing in the morning; for someone else, before lunch; for a third person, before bedtime; and for yet another person, it may best be done by awakening in the middle of the night.

By keeping the same time each day you can take advantage of a principle about the nature of the human mind: Your mind can be trained to make a change in consciousness at the same time each day. For example, you have probably already discovered that it's possible to train your mind to awaken at a particular time each morning to get ready for work. In this case, the training is to make the change in consciousness from the sleep state to the normal waking state. But the same principle can be used for moving from the normal waking state to the consciousness achieved in meditation. By keeping the same time each day for your meditation period, in effect you begin each meditation period "with a running start."

How long should your initial efforts at meditation last? A good length for beginners is just three or four minutes of silence. At first, even such a brief period will seem inordinately long. Yet with practice, you will get used to longer periods of keeping attention focused. Most meditators find that they want to build to at least 20-minute meditation periods. However, let such a length of meditation build up over the course of many weeks, increasing at a pace that best fits your temperament.

Step 3. Maintain long-term attunement practices as an ongoing preparation. This procedure for meditation invites you to think of the technique as occupying more than just 15 or 20 minutes each day. In a sense, you are always getting ready for your next meditation period by the way you treat your physical body, by what you feed your mind.

Each meditator needs to design a personalized kind of preparation program. Consider the way you treat your physical body as an essential ingredient to more effective meditation periods. Everyone has experienced the way changes in diet affect both mood and attention span. The simplest example of this can be observed after eating a large meal. A body preoccupied with digestion finds it difficult to stay consciously alert. However, the subtle effects of diet are probably even more important. Many meditators find that the elimination of certain food substances is crucial to optimal meditating (e.g., eliminating or minimizing sugar, caffeine, alcohol, etc.). Each person must decide from careful experimentation what kind of diet preparation works best.

Most meditators also find that a regular physical exercise program becomes an ongoing kind of meditation preparation. Again it's important to determine what fits your lifestyle, but activities such as running, swimming, yoga, or walking are highly recommended for most people.

Each meditator should also identify ways of thinking that can be either an enhancement or an obstacle to meditation. For example, if you hold resentful feelings toward an individual, until that pattern is changed, it constitutes a stumbling block toward more effective meditation periods. Of course, we should continue to meditate even though we have not cleansed ourselves totally of attitudinal and emotional stresses. However, the more we are able to monitor what we feed the soul through our daily attitudes and emotions, the better chance we have to obtain the deeper levels possible in meditation. As a first step in this kind of preparatory effort, identify just one or two attitudes or emotions that particularly need conscious work. Then *do* the necessary work!

Step 4. Just before each meditation session, use your own helpful aids for attunement. Here again, select those disciplines and activities that work best for you based on personal experimentation. Most meditators find that, when they first sit down to begin the meditation session, they still need some activities to help them enter the silence, even if they have been engaged in ongoing preparation (Step 3).

One kind of pre-meditation aid involves the physical body. For example, the Edgar Cayce readings recommend a simple head and neck exercise be done at the beginning of meditation. This exercise seems to alleviate much of the stress and tension we store in our necks and shoulders:

1. Sit up straight and let your head drop forward slowly, and then bring it slowly back upright. Do this three times.

2. Next, slowly move your head as far back as you can comfortably move it, and then slowly return your head to an upright position, a total of three times.

3. Next, do three similiar head movements to the right side.

4. Then, do three to the left side.

5. The exercise concludes with three circular movements of the head, first in a clockwise direction, and then in a counter-clockwise direction.

Another aid for attunement many meditators find helpful is to work with breathing. Although lengthy, somewhat forced deep breathing exercises are possible, it's also easy to use a more gentle approach to the breath. The simplest technique is to spend one or two minutes simply letting all of your attention dwell upon your breathing without trying to change the rate or depth of each breath. In other words, attention to the breath becomes a method for beginning to focus attention. Seemingly quite simple, this powerful technique is highly recommended.

Some meditators use a form of quieting or inspirational music at the beginning of meditation to evoke feelings of calm and uplifted spirits. Experiment with different kinds of music to find something that works for you. Some individuals also find that chanting is helpful at the start of a meditation session. Similarly, burning incense may create a physical stimulus that helps to both center the mind and evoke desired feelings.

Step 5. Begin with prayer. Remember that prayer and meditation are complementary. Beginning a meditation program for yourself does not reduce the importance and helpfulness of a prayer life. The two aid each other.

Spend several minutes in prayer before you begin to meditate. Remember that prayer is an activity of the conscious mind, whereas in meditation you will try to still the conscious mind. So during this prayer period let your conscious thought be active, but highly purposeful and directed. You may like to work with a prayer of thanksgiving, a prayer of petition, a prayer of praise, or a prayer of confession.

Many people working from a Christian orientation find this an especially appropriate place to work with the Lord's Prayer. The Edgar Cayce readings, for example, strongly encourage meditators to use the Lord's Prayer before beginning the silence period. The readings encourage us to say the prayer slowly, feel the meaning of each part of the prayer as it quickens and awakens a higher state of consciousness within the physical body.

Step 6. Repeat silently or aloud an affirmation corresponding to your spiritual ideal. Here "affirmation" is roughly equivalent to the Sanskrit "mantra." That is, the words chosen as a focus for attention need to have a powerfully evocative quality — able to awaken within us strong feelings of the ideal.

What words should you choose for your affirmation? You may take a favorite line from the Bible (e.g., "Be still and know that I am God") or from other sacred scripture. Or you may write your own short affirmation which encapsulates your spiritual ideal. Some meditators keep their affirmation quite brief and in fact use the short phrase they have selected to designate their spiritual ideal.

You may also find it helpful at the beginning of your meditation session to create in your mind some visual imagery that relates to your affirmation and helps you get in touch with it. For example, some meditators find it helpful to imagine themselves sitting in a special spiritual place. The image of that setting then allows them to identify more quickly with the life purpose which the affirmation represents.

Step 7. Focus your attention on the words of the affirmation and any images you're using, until you begin to experience the feeling and spirit behind the words. In this step, you are directing your conscious will to concentrate and keep your attention one-pointed. However, the effort you make to direct attention is not an intellectual effort to dissect the affirmation or analyze the images. Instead, let your attention rest upon the feeling and spirit the affirmation begins to call forth from your unconscious mind. This stage may require much practice because of the strong tendency for your attention to drift off to distracting thoughts and emotions.

Step 8. Release any images and the words of the affirmation and hold gently to their feeling or spirit. Once you have reached a point where you recognize that the affirmation has begun to do its work — that new feelings are being awakened — then drop the words and any images you have created. This is the silence of meditation. Here you rest in silent attention in the quiet spirit of the ideal your affirmation represents. At this point, words are unnecessary. They have done their job by getting you back in touch with another way of feeling and seeing yourself and life.

Step 9. When your attention drifts repeat Steps 7 and 8. In other words, you can expect that your capacity to stay in the silence will be limited. At first, you will probably find, after just 10 or 15 seconds of silently holding the feeling of your affirmation, that a distracting thought or emotion will grab your attention and pull you away. When you recognize you have been caught up in a distraction, go back to Step 7 and once again hold the words of the affirmation and/or image related to them in your attention until you re-experience their meaning and spirit. You may have to repeat this sequence many times in a single meditation session. Even experienced meditators have to go back frequency and reawaken to their sense of highest purpose by recalling the affirmation and then reattaining the silence.

Step 10. Surrender all efforts to make something happen. Steps 6 through 9 include effort on your part to direct the meditation session. Even if you have no expectations or desires for some special experience in meditation, conscious effort and the exercise of will is necessary in Steps 6 through 9.

However, the last phase of your meditation should include a short period during which you fully surrender, discontinuing all conscious effort. When you have spent sufficient time holding in silent attention the feeling and meaning of your affirmation, and you feel permeated by its spirit, release even the affirmation.

A good way to experience the surrender called for in Step 10 is to refocus your attention on your breathing. In other words, once you have let the meaning of your affirmation permeate both your conscious and unconscious, then spend several minutes in attentive breathing. This breathing exercise at the close is not to alter your breathing or to attempt to force a change in consciousness by an extraordinary breathing technique. Instead, by letting your attention focus on something as simple as your breath, the power of what you have subconsciously achieved in the previous steps is able to touch you even more deeply.

The key to this tenth step is the word "surrender." There must be a sense of giving up (but not of "giving in") — letting go of all mental efforts to force something to happen.

Step 11. Conclude by praying for others. This will be the closing for most meditation sessions. After you experience the release and the silence of meditation and feel a rejuvenating and an inner awakening, share what you have received through prayer. Since energy is directed by conscious intention and thought, through prayer for healing we can bless others for whom we have concern.

Unless a person has specifically asked you for prayer surround with light the individual about whom you have concern. In so doing, you provide an energy and even a state of consciousness the person can draw upon when ready to make changes in his or her life. On the other hand, if someone has asked you specifically to pray for his or her own healing of a particular condition, then it's appropriate to pray for specific changes in the person's life. Always add to each of your prayers some form of "God's will be done." This distinction between prayers for individuals for whom we have concern and prayers for individuals who have asked for such help is meant to insure a respect for the free will of each individual soul.

* * *

We have presented 11 steps in a "universal" approach to the meditation process, stopping along the way to explain and illustrate each of them. To feel the "flow" of these steps — especially Steps 4 through 11 — review them now as a continuous series of actions, each step moving smoothly and in its own time to the next:

1. Set a spiritual ideal for your life.

2. Set and maintain a consistent time of day for meditation.

3. Maintain long-term attunement practices as an ongoing preparation.

4. Just before each meditation session use your own helpful aids for attunement.

5. Begin with prayer.

6. Repeat silently or aloud an affirmation corresponding to your spiritual ideal.

7. Focus your attention on the words of the affirmation and any images you are using.

8. Release any images and the words of the affirmation, and hold gently to their feeling or spirit.

9. When your attention drifts, repeat Steps 7 and 8.

10. Surrender all efforts to make something happen.

11. Conclude by praying for others.

Do you have any expectations about what will happen during meditation — perhaps between Steps 10 and 11? Many people do, and so the next chapter deals with the meditation experience itself.

Chapter 4
What to Expect During Meditation

The beginning meditator may be disappointed by the infrequency of unusual experiences during meditation periods. Expectations may have been built from a report of remarkable experiences by others, or from assumptions about what will happen when we "encounter the infinite."

The "baseline" experience, as it were, is *stillness* in both body and mind. This quality begins with the absence of conscious thought or conscious reaction to the immediate environment, and the lack of bodily movement. Stillness may include a sense of "being" — an awareness beyond words of one's existence in the present moment. Regular meditators report experiencing stillness during most meditation periods.

Beyond the common experience of stillness, many meditators and teachings are in agreement as to some types of other experiences that *may* arise in meditation. These include:

1. The meditator reports *losing consciousness of the body*. Often this is described as a feeling of being suspended above the body, or as a complete inability to contact

physical sensations:

> When the desire for silence comes, not a single thought arises; he who is looking inward suddenly forgets that he is looking. At this time, body and heart must be left completely released. All entanglements have disappeared without trace. Then I no longer know at what place the house of my spirit and my crucible are. If a man wants to make certain of his body, he cannot get at it. This condition is the penetration of heaven into earth, the time when all wonders return to their roots. (Wilhelm, 1962, p. 56)

Cayce warns that one should not *attempt* to get out of the body during meditation (although one may lose all contact with physical sensations), since the purpose for this activity is to bring the consciousness of the infinite *into* the finite, physical expression (Cayce Reading 1782-1).

2. The meditator reports an experience of *contact or union with God*. These reports vary somewhat, and Govinda points out that each of us will experience the infinite in terms of our own needs:

> Those who suffer from bondage and confinement, will experience liberation as infinite expansion. Those who suffer from darkness, will experience it as light unbounded. Those who groan under the weight of death and transitoriness, will feel it as eternity. Those who are restless, will enjoy it as peace and infinite harmony. (Govinda, 1969, p. 24)

3. The meditator reports *speaking in tongues* (or "glossolalia"). Stanford states that such individuals are always in a state of emotional (if not spiritual) excitation" (1977, p. 115). The kundalini energies rise until they reach the thyroid (throat chakra); however, because of imperfections of the conscious ideal and the lack of cleansing of the bodily consciousness, the energy manifests at this level through the voice. In some cases, it draws upon the unlimited knowledge of the pineal center and the words spoken are actually of a language unknown to the conscious mind. In other cases, it is pure garble from the levels of the subcon-

scious.

4. The meditator reports *experiencing the Void*. However, this Void is not empty blackness, but a state of awareness pregnant with all the potentialities of life. Govinda quotes an ancient teacher to make this point:

. . . the potentiality of the Great Void . . . is so beauti-
fully expressed in the poetical words of the Sixth Patri-
arch . . . of the Ch'an School:

"When you hear me speak about the void, do not fall
into the idea that I mean vacuity. It is of the utmost
importance that we should not fall into that idea, because then when a man sits quietly and keeps his
mind blank, he would be abiding in a state of the
'voidness of indifference.' The illimitable void of the
universe is capable of holding myriads of things of
various shapes and forms . . ." (Govinda, 1969, p. 117)

5. The meditator reports *multi-dimensional experiences* that cannot be described in logical terms. Govinda compares these to a stereoscopic picture in which a higher degree of reality is achieved by the combination of two different points of view. Similiarly, an "experience of higher dimensionality is achieved by integration of experiences of different centers and levels of consciousness" (Govinda, 1969, p. 136). Yet, these experiences cannot be explained to a lesser, three dimensional consciousness which imposes distinct limits upon expression.

6. The meditator reports *the experience of brilliant, white light*. Underhill notes this phenomenon in the lives of nearly all mystics; Bucke lists it as one of the characteristics of cases of "Cosmic Consciousness." A possible explanation for this experience will be offered in Chapter 8 in the section on the pituitary gland. The light is the experience of the union of the infinite nature of man with the finite. In his commentary on *The Secret of the Golden Flower*, Jung refers to this light as the symbol of the Tao:

The unity of these two, life and consciousness, is
the Tao, whose symbol would be the central white light
. . . This light dwells in the "square inch," or in the

"face," that is, between the eyes (Jung, 1962, p. 103)

* * *

Having identified a variety of experiences that may be encountered in meditation, we must repeat and extend the point made at the beginning of this chapter: The meditator should not anticipate any specific experience and thus be disappointed when it does not occur. The experiences described in this chapter are presented so that, *if* any of them *do* start happening in your meditation life, you can realize you are not alone, nor is something wrong. Furthermore, meditators should not evaluate the "quality" of their meditation according to the frequency or kinds of special experiences they have during meditation.

In Chapter 1, we talked about entering meditation with a sense of *giving* of oneself, rather than with the idea of getting specific benefits — or experiences — from meditation. Again we suggest evaluating your meditation by asking yourself, "How deeply did I experience giving myself to something higher than myself?"

Chapter 5
How to Use Meditation for Guidance

Once you have begun a regular commitment to meditation, you may occasionally add another phase to some meditation sessions: You can receive inner guidance concerning specific decisions and problems in your life. Within you is a level of consciousness — an inner resource of wisdom — that can offer helpful instruction and solution to specific challenges you face. Pointing to this inner possibility, the Edgar Cayce readings state that the highest form of psychic perception is the inner contact each of us can make with the Spirit:

"Q-1. What is the highest possible psychic realization . . .?

A-1. That God, the Father, speaks directly to the sons of men — even as He has promised." (Cayce Reading 440-4)

Many people shy away from using meditation as a source of help for making decisions. Something within us makes us skeptical of inner promptings. We worry that we might make catastrophic decisions or be led astray by subjective illusions. However, if you are clear about what you are looking for, then the likelihood of misunderstanding or misinterpretation is much less.

Choose your approach to guidance according to the type of guidance you want — whether you seek an answer, additional information, or a confirmation. One approach is to seek guidance which provides a specific *answer* to a specific question. For example, you might pose to your inner consciousness questions such as, "Should I keep taking my medication despite its side effects?" or "Should I finally tell my next door neighbor what's been irritating me about his behavior for the past six months?" or "What new type of vocation should I explore?" In each of these instances, the exact *answer itself* is sought.

A second approach to guidance is to search for additional *information* so you can formulate an answer at a later time. With this technique, you reserve the role of final decision making for your conscious life, but ask your unconscious self to give you more facts or additional perspectives which might lead to a better answer. Examples of questions following this approach include, "What's my boss really feeling which leads to his actions that are so confusing to me?" or "What kind of past life experiences have I had with Richard which make me so attracted to him?" In these examples, the seeker is hoping to arrive eventually at a decision on how to act toward the boss, or how deeply to get involved with Richard. Yet inner guidance is sought only to provide the information that might lead to a better conscious decision.

The third strategy for seeking guidance involves looking for *confirmation* of a tentative conscious decision. In this instance the seeker looks for an inner sense of affirmation *or* warning concerning an intended course of action. For instance, one might pose these questions to the inner self: "Will it be best for my daughter if I follow through on the decision to enroll her in a private school?" or "Is the best financial result to be expected from following through on the planned sales of my automotive stock?"

None of these three approaches is clearly superior to

another for all situations, although some situations will be more suited to one of the three approaches. The Edgar Cayce readings most often encourage the use of the second and third approaches. In other words, the seeker should be careful about turning the entire decision-making process over to the unconscious and relying upon it alone for the answer to questions.

Another way to say this: God wants us to learn how to make decisions. In the Divine Plan for humanity, the personal will is to be awakened and used in a constructive manner. And yet paradoxically, it is in our best interests spiritually to befriend and cooperate with an unconscious Will always available to direct us wisely. The paradoxical nature of this principle can be frustrating to the seeker. Yet we arrive at the best approach for attuned decision making when we find a balance between two kinds of will — the conscious personal capacity to choose and the deeper understanding of a Transpersonal Will within the unconscious.

The following nine-step technique is one framework in which to experience such a creative balance:

Step 1. Set your spiritual ideal. This is the same as Step 1 in Chapter 3 on how to meditate. Any time you plan to use meditation as a method for getting inner guidance, take time to review the wording of your spiritual ideal and ask yourself whether or not those words still represent the spirit of living to which you aspire.

Step 2. Feel the readiness of a question to be answered. The following seven steps will work only if the question you are considering is one you are ready to have answered. In other words, there is a *rightness of timing* for virtually any life challenge. The seeker must be sensitive to when a question is still in the process of emerging and when the timing is right for an answer. When you feel really ready to learn the best way to approach some problem, then the time is right to proceed to the third step.

Step 3. Carefully formulate a wording for the question. At Step 2, the challenge or difficulty being reviewed may still be somewhat vague, but at this third step, you must formulate a specific wording for the issue. On paper, write out what you seek to know. Clarify for yourself whether you're looking for a direct answer, more information, or confirmation of something you're already inclined to do.

Step 4. Consider all the factors bearing on this question that you have some current knowledge about. This step involves working with the conscious mind to list all information relevant to your question. Suppose your question was "Should I move to Arizona?" In this fourth step, you would list all relevant information you already have, such as feelings of other family members about a move, job prospects in Arizona, considerations concerning the climate, employment possibilities, etc.

Step 5. Arrive at a tentative conscious decision. Using rational common sense as well as your own intuition, weigh all the factors listed in Step 4, and formulate a preliminary answer to your question. Make sure that the tentative answer is in keeping with your spiritual ideal. Additional steps follow this one, but you need to feel good enough about your tentative answer to follow through on it without compromising your ideals.

Step 6. Obtain guidance concerning your tentative decision from "outer sources." At this stage, you may want to turn to a trusted friend or professional counselor for advice. Or, you may want to use such esoteric resources as psychic readings, astrological readings, numerology, or I Ching. Another form of outer guidance many seekers find helpful is the periodic occurence of synchronistic signs and life events which contain a quality of guidance. By themselves, such meaningful coincidences may not be a reliable source upon which to base an important decision. Yet once you arrive at a tentative conscious answer, synchronistic events may give you a feeling of confirmation or warning. These coincidental signs may take the form of things you read or hear about which, in an inexplicable way, seem to provide you with feedback on the issue you're concerned about.

For this sixth step, work only with those forms of outer

guidance you feel comfortable about. Individuals may differ widely in their choice of outer resources.

Step 7. Look for guidance coming from "inner resources." Many different avenues are available to each of us for tuning in to a higher wisdom and higher Will. Some people receive these inner promptings through imaginative reverie, and others find that dreams provide such guidance. But no matter what other avenues may be pursued, be sure to include meditation guidance as a resource.

Using meditation to receive guidance is quite simple. However, the seeker must not use his or her question as a kind of affirmation, but rather should complete all of the steps described in Chapter 3 (including prayer for others) *before* turning to the question or problem at hand. In other words, take several minutes at the *end* of your meditation period to quietly pose in your conscious mind, several times the question as you formulated it for Step 3 of this chapter. Hold the question in mind and feel your sincere desire to resolve this issue. Experience your openness to understand the question in whatever new light or with whatever required changes a deeper wisdom within you may offer.

After silently posing and contemplating the question, begin to *listen*. The listening must be broader than merely listening for a voice no matter how still or small. In fact, some people do receive guidance through an inward kind of auditory form (hence clairaudience as one form of psychic perception). However, most people receive their guidance in some way other than by actually hearing words. The listening process should encompass one's whole being. Listen with your body. Listen with your imaginative forces. Listen with that part of your mind which formulates new concepts and perspectives.

What should you expect to receive? Although individuals differ widely in how they experience guidance, people report the following types of inner response:

- A strong feeling or intuition of the rightness or wrongness of the tentative conscious answer (i.e., what emerged from Step 5).

- A strong feeling, intuition or image of what is likely to happen if the tentative decision is followed. In this case, the unconscious is not making any decision, but precognitively giving impressions of likely future events, leaving it to the conscious self to decide whether or not that is the desired result.
- A new, previously unconsidered solution. Although we may often hope for this result in seeking meditation guidance, it is not necessarily the most frequent result. A direct answer or solution is sometimes presented, but frequently it is merely a piece of the puzzle with the remaining parts left to be filled in by the conscious self. By way of analogy, imagine that you have asked a skilled mathematician to be your tutor in a difficult algebra course. Now you are stumped on one particular problem. The tutor doesn't provide you with the entire solution, but gives you a piece of the answer to get you started on finding the rest of the solution for yourself.
- Impressions which provide a new perspective on the current question or problem. In other words, the insight received in meditation may not answer the problem, but instead, suddenly allow you to see the question from a whole new angle. Sometimes this new view can then quickly lead to understanding the appropriate way to respond.
- Recognition of *another* question to be dealt with before the principal concern can be addressed. In other words, we may have posed a question we sincerely desire to have answered, and yet there are other issues to be resolved before it's possible to formulate the desired answer. Suppose you've posed the question, "Should I go back to graduate school to obtain further job skills?" In meditation, you may receive impressions not directly concerned with an answer to this question, but instead calling to mind other questions that must be resolved first, such as "Are you making the best use of the skills you currently have?" or "Have you resolved how you contribute to the dissatisfaction you feel with your current job situation?"

Before moving on to the next step, seek meditation guidance as described for Step 7 on more than one occasion for a single question, particularly for issues of great personal importance.

Step 8. Formulate a "guided" decision upon which you are ready to act. Take into account the input provided both from outer sources of guidance as well as inner guidance such as meditation. Then reconsider the question and write down a revised version of your answer — one that you're ready to begin to apply. Make sure this decision is something you could conceivably follow through on and still be in keeping with your spiritual ideal.

Step 9. Begin to apply the decision and yet respond constructively to obstacles which may arise. Almost invariably, when we begin to put into motion a decision (no matter how meditatively we may or may not have arrived at it), obstacles and resistances arise. Sometimes these obstacles can be traced directly to an origin within one's self, although most frequently we *experience* them as coming from outside. Of course, our hope is that the guided decision will be easy to bring to fruition. And yet seldom is this the case.

When such obstacles arise, the seeker is likely to respond in one of two non-productive ways:

- First, we tend to try bullheadedly to force our way through the obstacles. Something within us says, "I've gotten my guidance and now I'm going to *make* it happen, no matter what anyone else says or does!" This kind of stubbornness very rarely leads to a happy ending.
- The second frequent response is to give up. In other words, something within us expects that everything will quickly fall into place if we have tuned into a higher wisdom and this almost lazy part of ourselves doesn't want to have to make any persistent efforts.

A third alternative is a more productive way of responding to the natural obstacles which arise. It requires a willingness to persist in applying the guided decision and yet maintain an openness, so that the obstacles or resistances can teach us and help us to refine the guidance to a more applicable form. In other words, through meditation or any other form of guidance, we may have the basic *theme* of the best decision, and yet not have a proper understanding of the right *timing* or *way* in which to proceed, or of the *people* who will be involved in bringing the decision to fruition.

The best approach involves a careful blend of consistent effort with an open-mindedness that looks upon guidance as an *ongoing process* and not something that was resolved once and for all in Step 8. We must let life continue to instruct us. Continue to keep a regular meditation period as you apply your guided decisions. You can expect that signs and indicators and even further meditation guidance will continue to help you. This by-product of a regular meditation life is one of its most valuable fruits.

* * *

This chapter on guidance through meditation concludes the section on *practicing* meditation. Conscientious, regular effort in following the steps outlined in Chapters 3 and 5 will help any individual take important steps along the path of integrating the spiritual with the physical and mental through meditation.

This section has also discussed some fundamental principles underlying meditation, and the next section goes on to further enhance your *understanding* of the why's and how's of this process.

UNDERSTANDING MEDITATION

Chapter 6.   Who We Are

Chapter 7.   What Role Meditation Plays in Who We Are

Chapter 8.   What Happens in Our Bodies When We Meditate

Chapter 9.   How East Meets West in Meditation Tradition

Chapter 6
Who We Are

An approach to meditation, such as proposed in previous chapters, must have a rationale based on a thorough definition of the nature of human existence. Without such a foundation, meditation — dealing as it does with so many aspects of human nature — can be interpreted by many people as magic or cultish ritual with no objective validity. However, once we have agreed to embrace the fundamental concepts of the nature of our "humanness," as defined by the sources used in this book, the validity of universal aspects of meditation is more apparent, cutting across many cultures and traditions.

Most disagreements about theories or techniques — relating to education, child rearing, meditation, or whatever — can better be approached by first addressing the question, "As human beings, who are we?" Of course, this question cannot be answered simply. The sources for this book offer many concepts, each of which gives a partial answer. Together they create a comprehensive foundation for our approach to meditation. This statement of the nature of humanity consists of six points:

1. **All life — indeed, all that exists — is a manifestation of the one creative energy which is God.** All force is one force. Although the universe has only one energy, that energy manifests in many forms. For example, the energy of electricity and the energy that one uses when afraid is the same energy. The energy of an atomic reaction and the energy used in joyful enthusiasm are simply different manifestations of this one energy. We can easily fall into the illusion that we have a certain amount of work energy, a certain amount of sexual energy and a certain amount of anger energy, and we can believe that these energies can be expressed only in these particular forms. However, such a concept leads to a belief in many gods: a god of work, a god of love, a god of war, etc. Whenever we believe that we cannot transform energy that might be expressed negatively into a more creative or loving expression, we accept the notion of many gods. Contrast this with the awareness of the oneness of God.

Lama Govinda (1969, p. 64) refers to this principle in pointing out the discrepancy in appearance between a diamond and a lump of coal. However, both consist of the same chemical substance: carbon. This demonstrates the fundamental unity of all life and its inherent capacity for transformation:

> . . . all existing elements or phenomena are only variations of the same force or substance . . . Therefore, he who succeeds in penetrating to the purity of its undifferentiated primordial form, has gained the key to the secret of all creative power, which is based on the mutability of all elements and phenomena. (Govinda, 1969, p. 51)

> For all force, all power that is manifested in thyself, is of the ONE source. (Cayce Reading, 1494-1)

2. **Every individual is a spiritual being, yet is not aware of the totality of that being.** We have projected ourselves into a lesser dimension, a more limited state of consciousness that can be described as three-dimensional. We measure our experience in terms of three variables: (a) when an

experience happens (time), (b) where it happens (space), and (c) the degree of understanding we have or the response we make to the experience. The Cayce readings (e.g., Reading 262-114) refer to this third dimension as "patience."

Often we describe the world as having the three dimensions of length, width, and depth. Time is commonly spoken of as the fourth dimension. However, in this system, length, width, and depth are sub-dimensions of space, while time has the sub-dimensions of past, present and future.

Because we operate in a three-dimensional frame of reference, we tend to perceive or conceptualize in threes. For example, we see ourselves as having a body, mind, and spirit (or soul). Many understand the Godhead as a trinity (e.g., in Christianity, the Father, the Son and the Holy Spirit). The triune concept is based upon an underlying unity, but because we are in this particular dimension of awareness, it is helpful for us to deal with these triune concepts in many of our beliefs and perceptions.

Several sources used in this book provide examples of this three-part conceptualization. The Cayce readings (e.g., Reading 900-16) refer to the mind as consisting of the superconscious (the part still in contact with the infinite), the subconscious (the storehouse of memory of all experiences), and the conscious (or waking, physical consciousness). This has been interpreted in the model shown in Fig. 1 (Puryear and Thurston, 1978, p. 24).

The Secret of the Golden Flower describes three levels of man's activity which have been interpreted as eros, intuition and logos:

> The way to the Elixir of Life knows as supreme magic, seed-water, spirit-fire, and thought-earth: these three. What is seed-water? It is the true, one energy of former heaven (eros). Spirit-fire is the light (logos). Thought-earth is the heavenly heart of the middle dwelling (intuition). (Wilhelm, 1962, pp. 25-26)

Govinda presents a three-part model that is very similar. Writing about the spiritual centers of the body (to be dis-

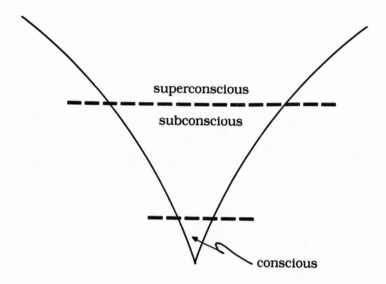

Fig. 1. A Model of the Nature of Humanity

cussed in Chapter 8), he categorizes their activity into three sections:

These three zones represent in their deepest sense:

1. The terrestrial plane, namely, that of earth-bound elementary forces of nature, or materiality or corporeality . . .;

2. The cosmic or universal plane of eternal laws, of timeless knowledge . . . a plane of spontaneous spiritual awareness of the Infinite . . .;

3. The human plane of individual realization, in which . . . the forces of the earth and of the universe which become conscious in the human soul as an ever-present and *deeply felt* reality. (Govinda, 1969, p. 175)

The first zone may be compared to "seed-water" and the "conscious mind"; the second zone, to "spirit-fire" and the "superconscious mind"; and the third zone, to "thought-earth" and the "subconscious mind."

As spiritual beings, we were meant to experience lesser dimensions in consciousness and to bring the qualities of our spiritual nature fully into manifestation in these limited states of awareness. The "fall of man" — representing our descent into a materialized sense of ourselves — is not really a spatial description, but a process of awareness focusing more and more upon material forms and sensations associated with the body, and the exclusion of awareness related to the spiritual or infinite aspect of being. We find ourselves with a sense of our own dual nature: as an individual of the spirit and as an individual of the earth. This dual nature is described in *The Secret of the Golden Flower*:

Each individual contains a central monad, which, at the moment of conception, splits into life and human nature, *ming* and *hsing*. These two are supra-individual principles, and so can be related to eros and logos.

In the personal bodily existence of the individual they are represented by two other polarities, a *p'o* soul (or anima) and a *hun* soul (animus). All during the life of the individual these two are in conflict, each striving for mastery . . .

If the life-energy flows downward, that is, without let or hindrance into the outer world, the anima is victorious over the animus; no spirit-body or Golden Flower is developed, and at death the ego is lost. If the life-energy is led through the "backward-flowing" process, that is, conserved, and made to "rise" instead of allowed to dissipate, the animus has been victorious, and the ego persists after death. (Wilhelm, 1962, pp. 64-65)

Our work on earth is to re-experience the full consciousness of our own infinite nature, brought about only as we bring the awareness of the infinite *into* the finite. It is not enough for us to run away from our limitations and humanness to embrace the infinite, or to seek a way by which our own finite nature can be swallowed in an ocean of Oneness. The real goal is expressed by Govinda and by Stanford:

. . . Edwin Arnold's "Light of Asia" ends with the words: "The dew-drop slips into the shining sea." If this beautiful simile is reversed, it would probably come nearer to the Buddhist conception of ultimate realization: it is not the drop that slips into the sea, but the sea that slips into the drop! The universe becomes conscious in the individual (but not vice versa) . . . (Govinda, 1969, p. 81)

Some have said that the uniqueness of Christ as Jesus was that a man became conscious of God, that an individual became conscious of God. But we would now give a greater significance: *God became conscious as an individual!* This is why you are in the earth — not to become conscious of God, for you were that before entering the earth. Not that, as many religions and peoples believe, but that God would become conscious *as man*, that God would become an individual. There is a difference. One is a transformation, an amelioration, the purpose for which he entered.The

other is, well, merely returning the pancake to its bat-
ter. (Stanford, 1976, p. 200)

The process of the infinite expressing in the finite must
begin at the point in consciousness in which we find ourselves. To reverse the descent into matter, Govinda advises,
we must proceed in the reverse order in which we came to
the present state. He warns against trying to achieve the
infinite state of being before we have done all we can to
attune and purify the finite aspects of body and mind. Not
that one should ignore the spiritual dimension of seeking
and work only on the physical and mental. As discussed
in Chapter 1, setting a spiritual ideal before beginning any
attempt to transform the body and mind is very important.
Instead, Govinda cautions us to beware of two related temp-
tations: (1) to assume that we may leave behind the finite
expressions of our being (which we have built in the earth),
and (2) to hope to find ourselves on the top of the mountain
without having traversed its foot.

3. **Any time the one energy is expressed in the physical
world, it will have form patterned by the mind.** The energy
takes on a pattern, shape, or vibration, given to it by the
mind. As the one energy is given a form, we can begin to
speak of it objectively or refer to a thought as a thing. The
mental activity called "desire" creates a vibrational pattern
with the one energy that is just as *real* as acting out the
desire in the material world:

For, thoughts are things! and they have their effect
upon individuals, especially those that become super-
sensitive to outside influences! These are just as physical as sticking a pin in the hand! (Cayce Reading
386-2)

And so, mind is the mediator between the pure, life-giv-
ing energy and its manifestation — between the spirit and
the physical. With the mind, we can modify the way this
energy is expressed in the earth. As the mediator, mind
partakes of both that which is temporal and that which is
eternal — of the finite nature of the physical body and the
infinite nature of Spirit. Referring to this principle, Go-

vinda provides the following statement, illustrated in Fig. 2:

> Manas [mind] is that element of our consciousness which holds the balance between the empirical-individual qualities on the one side and the universal-spiritual qualities on the other. It is that which either binds us to the world of the senses or which liberates us from it. (Govinda, 1969, p. 75)

Thus our work in being in the earth is to bring the infinite or spiritual into manifestation in the three-dimensional world. Being the mediator between the two, the mind is the primary agent of transformation.

4. **The patterning activities of the mind can be understood as being fourth-dimensional.** We find this concept in both the Cayce readings and in the writings of Carl Jung:

> Best definition that ever may be given of the fourth dimension is an idea! Where will it project? Anywhere! Where does it arise from? Who knows! Where will it end? Who can tell! It is all inclusive! It has both length, breadth, height and depth — is without beginning and is without ending! (Cayce Reading 364-10)

> If we wished to form a vivid picture of a non-spatial being of the fourth dimension, we should do well to take thought, as a being, for our model. (Jung, 1933, p. 213)

In this way, the three-dimensional world can be interpreted as a projection of the fourth dimension. The principle here is that something projected takes on a lesser dimension. For example, in spatial dimensions, if we shine a flashlight on a basketball in such a way that the shadow of the ball appears on the wall, the darkened circle we see is a two-dimensional projection of the three-dimensional ball. In a similar manner, what we perceive in our three-dimensional world can be understood as a projection of the fourth dimension, the realm of thoughts or ideas. From this point of view, we can say that consciousness, as we know it, is a *past* condition. That is, what we see as our material world is the *result* of mental processes that took

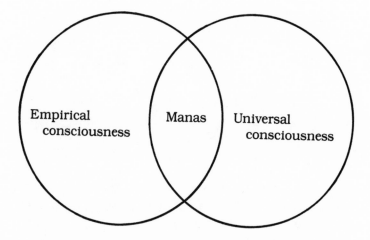

Fig. 2. The Relationship of Manas to Empirical
Consciousness and Universal Consciousness

place before that time. In Govinda's words:

What appears as form does thus belong essentially to the past, and is therefore felt as alien by those who have developed spiritually beyond it ... (Govinda, 1969, p. 69)

What we experience now as reality is, in actuality, the manifestation of what we have built previously. As with an architect's blueprints, once the blueprint has been drawn, we know what the building will look like when it manifests. It is only a matter of transforming it from its idea level into physical manifestation. We can go back and modify our thought patterns — modify the blueprints — but unless we do, the nature of the manifestation is fixed. Fourth-dimensional reality, therefore, is at the creating level. Something that manifests in the three-dimensional world is already a past condition, relatively speaking. Govinda summarizes this concept with the principle:

Materialization can be influenced, directed and modified only while it is still in the process of formation. (Govinda, 1969, p. 215)

5. **Every individual has will, by which to choose how to use the patterning qualities of the mind.** Attaining the infinite in the finite requires the use of the will. We must *choose* to operate under the direction of the infinite aspect of our being, as opposed to our limited aspects. No other influence is stronger than the will:

To be born as a human being is a privilege, according to the Buddha's teaching, because it offers the rare opportunity of liberation through one's own decisive effort, through a "turning about in the deepest seat of consciousness." (Govinda, 1969, p. 124)

Q. Are hereditary, environment and will equal factors in aiding or retarding the entity's development?

A. Will is the greater factor, for it may overcome any or all of the others; provided that will is made one with the pattern, see? For, no influence of heredity, environment or what not, surpasses the will ... (Cayce Reading 5749-14)

For the will of each entity, of each soul, is that which individualizes it, that makes it aware of itself . . . (Cayce Reading 853-9)

As to what an entity does concerning its environs or hereditary influence from the *material* viewpoint, this is governed by the action of the will (that active principle making for the *individuality* of an entity, from those atomic forces that may manifest in a material plane or in *any* sphere of material or matter existence). Thus is *man* endowed with the individual soul.

Hence the *will* is an *attribute* of the soul, and the whole development of an entity. (Cayce Reading 274-1)

6. **Enlightenment comes from the integration of the various aspects of our being.** We must understand that form and spirit are equally important to our purpose for being in the earth. The rejection of the body cannot lead to the attainment of the infinite in the finite:

. . . Those . . . who only suppress their sense-activities and natural functions of life, before they even have tried to make the right use of them, will not become saints but merely petrefacts. A saintliness, which is built merely on negative virtues, merely on avoidance and escape, may impress the crowd and may be taken as proof of self-control and spiritual strength; however, it will lead only to spiritual self-annihilation, but not to Enlightenment. (Govinda, 1969, p. 273)

* * *

We have been addressing the question of who we are as human beings, or — putting it another way — what is the nature of being human? The answer has been in the form of six points:

1. All life — indeed, all that exists — is a manifestation of the one creative energy which is God.

2. Every individual is a spiritual being, yet is not aware of the totality of that being.

3. Any time the one energy is expressed in the physical world, it will have form, patterned by the mind.

4. The patterning activities of the mind can be un-

derstood as being fourth-dimensional.

5. Every individual has will, by which to choose how to use the patterning qualities of the mind.

6. Enlightenment comes from the integration of the various aspects of our being.

All this may seem to be far from the concerns of meditation. Quite the contrary, meditation is a critical skill for each of us if we are to come to grips with who we are collectively, and especially if we are seeking to discover ourselves individually. The next chapter connects the concepts of meditation with the concepts of our humanness, our presence in this world, our reasons for being.

Chapter 7
What Role Meditation Plays in Who We Are

The Pattern to be Awakened

In the preceding chapter, we saw how we impart form qualities to the one energy with our mind. That form or vibrational pattern created by the mind (at the fourth-dimensional level) can hinder or aid greater self-awareness, depending upon its nature. That suggests we must be wise in our choice of pattern to create. Therefore, we must identify those patterns most conducive to achieving the integrated self we seek for enlightenment. At the fourth-dimensional level, we have access to every thought we have ever created. In addition, we have access to patterns that are shared or common to all humankind. These impersonal or archetypal patterns manifest in the dreams and the myths of all cultures. Differentiating between patterns that have been individually created (based upon our unique experiences or choices) and those patterns which are available to all, Jung writes:

A more or less superficial layer of the unconscious is undoubtedly personal. I call it the *personal uncon-*

scious. But this personal unconscious rests upon a deeper layer, which does not derive from personal experience and is not a personal acquisition but is inborn. This deeper layer I call the *collective unconscious.* I have chosen the term "collective" because this part of the unconscious is not individual but universal; in contrast to the personal psyche, it has contents and modes of behavior that are more or less the same everywhere and in all individuals. It is, in other words, identical in all men and thus constitutes a common psychic substrate of a suprapersonal nature which is present in every one of us.

. . .The contents of the collective unconscious are known as *archetypes.* (Jung, 1959, p. 3)

In his investigation of symbology, Govinda comes to a similar conclusion:

While mantric symbols have their origin within the cultural realm of a certain language or civilization, there are other symbols of figurative and conceptual nature, the origin of which cannot be traced to any particular place, tribe, or race, and which are not bound to any particular period of human civilization or to any religion, but which are the common property of humanity. These symbols may disappear in one place — in fact they may be buried for centuries — only to reappear at another place, and to rise resurrected in a new and more brilliant garb. They may change their names and even their meaning, according to the emphasis laid upon the one or the other of their aspects, without losing their original direction: because it is in the nature of a symbol to be as manifold as the life from which it grew, and yet to retain its character, its organic unity within the diversity of its aspects. (Govinda, 1969, p. 51)

One of these archetypal patterns within the unconscious is consistent with an integrated state of being — the goal toward which we strive — in which the infinite expresses through the finite. Diverse elements of consciousness are drawn together in this pattern — heart and head, feeling and intellect, highest love and deepest knowledge. This highest archetype is within each of us, not only in the sense that we can experience it visually (as in a dream), but in terms of a functioning of the entire body in a healed and integrated fashion.

The Cayce readings refer to the following qualities of this pattern and its expression: relevant to *human* experience, available to every individual, service, seeing God in every expression, obedient to the inner law, humor, compassion for others, living in the present, forgiveness, patience, humility, and the emphasis upon the importance of the spirit in which one acts. The activity of this pattern in one's life is initiated as one manifests these qualities.

Jung calls this pattern *the Christ archetype.* He argues that the rapid spread of Christianity is evidence to support his notion that the Christ is an element of the collective unconscious, and hence available to all:

Christ would never have made the impression He did on His followers if He had not expressed something that was alive and at work in their unconscious. Christianity itself would never have spread through the pagan world with such astonishing rapidity had its ideas not found an analagous psychic readiness to receive them. It is this fact which also makes it possible to say that whoever believes in Christ is not only contained in Him, but that Christ then dwells in the believer as the perfect man formed in the image of God. . . .(Jung, 1958, p. 441)

The Cayce readings refer to it as *the Christ consciousness.* The following reading is a concise description of our relationship to that pattern, including the important reference to the will. The Christ consciousness will remain a latent potential within the unconscious unless an individual exercises his will to choose it:

Q. Should the Christ-Consciousness be described as the awareness within each soul, imprinted in pattern on the mind and waiting to be awakened by the will, of the soul's oneness with God?

A. Correct. That's the idea exactly! (Cayce Reading 5749-14)

The Secret of the Golden Flower describes this pattern within us as something that existed before the creation of the world:

Within our six-foot body we must strive for the form which existed before the laying down of heaven and earth. (Wilhelm, 1962, p. 34)

Govinda points out that the movement of this pattern from a latent force to an active force transforms our concept of reality:

Bodhi-citta . . . is here the spark of that deeper consciousness, which in the process of enlightenment is converted from a latent into an active all-penetrating and radiating force. Before this awakening has taken place, our existence is a senseless running about in circles; and since we cannot find any meaning within ourselves, the world around us appears equally meaningless. (Govinda, 1969, p. 274)

Now that we are aware of the latent pattern within us, we can define "enlightenment" (just referred to by Govinda) as the process of awakening that pattern and, through will, keeping it at the center of our being. Meditation is the primary technique for facilitating that process.

The Process of Enlightenment

Sources comparing approaches to meditation describe many processes from which a meditator can choose. Naranjo describes three basic approaches:

The three types of meditation may be represented as the three points of a triangle. . . .At one end of the base line is represented meditation upon externally given symbolic objects, and at the other end is the contrasting alternative of meditation upon spontaneously arising contents of the mind. . . .

In the former approach the individual attempts to interiorize an externally given form, or projects his experience onto it, until his subjectivity is absorbed by the object. In the latter, the individual seeks attunement to an inner form or a formless depth out of which a personal form emerges — in imagery, thoughts, gestures, feelings, or, above all, as an attitude toward the situation at the moment. . . .

In contrast with these two orientations in the task of meditation — on outer-directed and the other inner-directed — the third point in our triangle stands for a pure *negative* approach: not a reaching out or a reaching in but a self-emptying. In this approach the effort is to attain a stillness of the mind's conceptualizing activity. (Naranjo & Ornstein, 1971, pp.16-17)

Seen in the light of teachings from other sources, we can conclude that a meditator will use more than one of these approaches. An individual may move from one approach to another over the course of many years of experience (e.g., learning concentration on an external symbol, before moving to symbols that arise from within); or the meditator may move from one approach to another within a single meditation period (e.g., focusing on an externally given object initially, and then moving into the total stillness of mind that characterizes the negative way).

Otto distinguishes between two pathways: the mysticism of introspection and the mysticism of unifying vision. The teaching of the former is "the secret way leads inward" — a withdrawal from all outward things, retreat into the ground of one's own being, and the possibility of turning in upon oneself. The teaching of the latter is "the unifying vision as opposed to the multiplicity of the object." It has no need for a doctrine of the soul but sees all being in terms of its fundamental oneness.

Otto points out that these two ways can be combined in the searchings of one individual. He quotes Plotinus to demonstrate this:

In Plotinus also both types of mysticism intermingle. The first is clearly expressed by him in a passage of the *Sixth Ennead:*

Often when I awake from the slumber of the body and come to myself, and step out of the outward world in order to turn in upon myself, I behold a wonderful beauty. Then I believe unshakeably that I belong to a better world; most glorious life works strongly in me and I am become one with the Godhead. . . .

But compare this passage with the following extract from the *Fifth Ennead, 8:*

They see all not in process of becoming but in Being, and they see themselves in the other. Each Being contains within itself the whole intelligible world. Therefore all is everywhere. Each is there all and all is each.

Man as he ceases to be an individual he raises himself again and penetrates the whole world. Then, become one with the All, he creates the All.
(Otto, 1932, pp. 59-60)

Many sources agree that the pathway to enlightenment is not just an ascension to states of awareness such as Otto describes above, or as Govinda described earlier, but must include a descent into the dark side of oneself so that this element of one's being may be included in any final integration. Naranjo describes the journey of self-exploration represented in Dante's wanderings through hell as "contemplation. . .not directed to symbolic embodiments of the spiritual goal" (Naranjo & Ornstein, 1971, p. 65). In such a process, one is merely an impartial observer of this aspect of oneself without judgment as to what is "good." Such a process leads to a reevaluation and new perspective of one's true nature.

Some approaches use symbolic forms to *awaken* the inhabitants of the dark side of the self. Such approaches assume that undesirable and destructive drives within us merely imbalanced conditions of something that is essentially good. Naranjo concludes that the archetypal images

used to personify and call up these forces serve as models
to direct them to their proper channels. Such images are
lacking in Western culture, which has generally been incap-
able of seeing God in madness and chaos. European Christianity has been primarily ascetic and has attempted to
reach God by transcending nature. The "Mystery religions"
and certain Greek figures (such as Dionysus and Per-
sephone) are some of the rare examples of the pathway of
descent in Western history.

Any discussion of the meditation process — be it the way
of ascent or descent — must be concerned more with inner
experience than with the technique that accompanies the
experience. Although the emphasis of our times is on
technique — the "how to's" — far more important to the
process of meditation is the way in which it is used. Sincer-
ity and devotion are the greatest tools of the meditator in
the search to know the God forces within, as well as those
of the universe beyond. Common to all schools of meditation is the definition of *what takes place in meditation:
the transformation of one's sense of identity.* That process
of transformation is described in different terms by the
Buddhist, the Taoist, and the Christian. Yet, important
parallels between these teachings emerge. As you review
these ideas from diverse sources, you will see the foundations for the "universal" approach to meditation described
in Chapter 3.

Tibetan Buddhism and meditation. Govinda's approach
to meditation is based upon the process symbolized by the
Great Mantra "Om Mani Padme Hum." These four seed syllables represent the states of progress towards enlightenment.

"Om" is the experience of the infinite within us:

In the experience of OM, man opens himself, goes
beyond himself, liberates himself, by breaking through
the narrow confines of egohood or self-imposed limita-
tion, and thus he becomes one with the All, with the
Infinite. If he would remain in this state, there would
be an end of his existence as an individual, as a living,

thinking and experiencing being. (Govinda, 1969, p. 129)

The "Om" is not the ultimate in the mantric system of Buddhism (as it is in some religions), but it stands at the beginning and is the fundamental experience for whoever seeks enlightenment.

"Mani" is the precious jewel within the mind of the individual, the goal of the alchemists, the symbol of the highest within man's mind. It may be compared to the Christ pattern or archetype latent within each of us.

That jewel within the mind can express itself as *form* and as creative vision. "Padme" comes from the Sanskrit word for lotus (padma) and involves the unfoldment of the latent spiritual consciousness in form:

This lotus represents the unfoldment of the perfect mind or the ideal Buddhahood, in which the qualities of Enlightenment or of the Buddha, which are the *sādhaka's* aim, are differentiated in visible form. (Govinda, 1969, p. 106)

"Hum" is the realization of the consciousness of the infinite in the finite. It is the penetration of the "Om" into the form that has been created:

OM is the ascent towards universality, HŪM the descent of the state of universality into the depth of the human heart. HŪM cannot be without OM. But HŪM is more than OM: it is the Middle Way which neither gets lost in the finite nor in the infinite, which is neither attached to the one nor to the other extreme.

Therefore it is said: "In darkness are they who worship only the world, but in greater darkness they who worship the infinite alone. He who accepts both saves himself from death by the knowledge of the former and attains immortality by the knowledge of the latter" *(Iśā Upaniṣad).* (Govinda, 1969, p. 130)

Govinda warns that meditation upon this mantra and the process that it embodies is not an analytical procedure, for that would serve only to entrap us further in an illusory concept of ourselves:

Meditation, through which we try to free ourselves from the empirical world by analytical methods of contemplation and intellectual dissection, gets us more and more involved in it, because instead of reversing the direction of our mind, we concentrate our whole attention upon the phenomena of this world, thus strengthening our own illusory conceptions of it. (Govinda, 1969, pp. 77-78)

The proper use of this mantra — "Om mani padme hum" — can awaken higher dimensions of awareness. Govinda recognizes that the state of consciousness in which one begins this process of enlightenment is threatened by the idea of higher dimensions of awareness taking over. The limited self fears annihilation and will come up with many excuses and distractions to protect itself and delay the changes of the meditative process. But such a fear is based on a misunderstanding of that process.

Thus the consciousness of a higher dimension consists in the coordinated and simultaneous perception of several. . .directions of movement, in a wider, more comprehensive unity, without destroying the individual characteristics of the integrated lower dimensions. The reality of a lower dimension is therefore not annihilated by a higher one, but only "relativized" or put into another perspective of values. (Govinda, 1969, p. 218)

The Lord's Prayer and meditation. The same process symbolized in the Great Mantra is represented in the Lord's Prayer of the Christian Bible. That four-fold progression is (a) a movement into the oneness of all being, (b) the awareness of the pattern or seed of that oneness within the individual mind, (c) the open and receptive form established, and (d) the penetration of the infinite *into* the finite.

"Our Father Who art in heaven" recognizes the oneness of the Godhead or the infinite. "Hallowed be Thy Name" refers to the Christ and that indwelling pattern (the Christ is associated with the Word, as in St. John's "the Word became flesh"). "Thy Kingdom come" expresses that openness and receptivity. "Thy Will be done in earth as it is in heaven" calls for the manifestation of the divine will in the material world.

This remarkable parallel between the Buddhist mantric tradition and the prayer which is at the heart of Christianity raises the possibility that this four-stage progression describes a process that is fundamental to the psyche of the human being and is more than just one culture's approach to enlightenment.

The Secret of the Golden Flower and meditation. Two unique phrases are used in this Taoist text to refer to the process of meditation. "The circulation of the light" refers to the movement of energy along the kundalini pathway. And yet, it is more than just the movement of energy because the possibility of "circulation without light" is raised. To clarify this, consider the statement in the text, "the light is contemplation." This suggests that the energy (awakened as the body becomes still) attains the *qualities of the light* as the mind focuses upon or *contemplates* the spiritual ideal. The details of the process involved in the circulation of the light are found in the following passage. Of particular interest is the meeting in the abdomen of the spirit with the rising kundalini. (This closely parallels material in the Stanford readings to be considered in the next chapter which describes a hormonal call from the pineal to awaken the energy at the cells of Leydig.)

If one wants to maintain the primal spirit one must, without fail, first subjugate the perceiving spirit. The way to subjugate it is through the circulation of the light. If one practices the circulation of the light, one must forget both body and heart. The heart must die, the spirit live. When the spirit lives, the breath will begin to circulate in a wonderful way. This is what the Master called the very best. Then the spirit must be allowed to dive down into the abdomen (solar plexus). The energy then has intercourse with spirit, and spirit unites with the energy and crystallizes itself. This is the method of starting the work. (Wilhelm, 1962, pp.

29-30)

A second unique phrase used by this text is "fixating contemplation." Fixation relates to the process of crystallizing or giving form (even in the physical body) to a pattern held by the mind. The text says that the light (or the ideal) "is easy to move, but difficult to fix" (Wilhelm, 1962, p. 22). If it is allowed to circulate for a long enough period of time, fixation can take place. The text at one point mentions 15 minutes as a minimum length of time for meditation. This may be the time required to overcome the difficulty of fixation.

These teachings go on with an often-quoted esoteric passage that describes the process of focusing on the ideal (contemplation) and of the distractions that may arise:

> Fixating contemplation is indispensable; it ensures the making fast of the enlightenment. Only one must not stay sitting rigidly if worldly thoughts come up, but one must examine where the thought is, where it began, and where it fades out. . .When the flight of the thoughts keeps extending further, one should stop and begin contemplating. Let one contemplate and then start fixating again. That is the double method of making fast the enlightenment. It means the circulation of the light. (Wilhelm, 1962, p. 36)

In the earlier discussions of meditation techniques, the use of an "affirmation" was defined as focusing on a representation of the ideal. If we substitute this term for the word "contemplation" and make other substitutions based upon relationships already described, the above passage may be rewritten more meaningful as follows:

> Meditation is invaluable to spiritual growth. It insures that enlightenment will not be just a fleeting or transitory experience. But don't become tense or frustrated if thoughts about daily life arise. Examine the thought and accept it. See where it began and where it fades out. If you catch yourself letting a train of worldly thoughts carry you further and further, stop and go back to the affirmation. Say the affirmation

again and then let it once more begin to be built or crystallized within you. That is the double method of making the enlightenment permanent. It means the movement of the one, creative energy throughout your being.

Rousselle's Study of Taoism and meditation. This material presents a four-part developmental progression that has many similarities to the stages symbolized in the Great Mantra and the Lord's Prayer. The first stage is the experience of the other pole. Tibetan Buddhism refers to the pole of the infinite, as opposed to the limited, ego sense of self. Rousselle describes the first stage as the experience of the *unconscious* pole, through the circulation of the light:

The first thing the novice must experience is the existence in the unconscious of an opposite center, in which he immerses himself on the one hand and which on the other hand he raises up into consciousness. This stage is called the "circulation of the light" or, to borrow a Buddhist expression — the "wheel of *dharma. . .,*" which must be "turned." (Rousselle, 1960, p. 88)

Once the opposite pole has been experienced, the second stage involves entering the path of transformation. Just as the "Mani" involves the awareness of the jewel or highest pattern within the individual's mind, Rousselle describes this stage as the awakening of the seed of the new, immortal man:

The novice who has reached the meditative experience of the third eye is indeed filled with an ecstatic sense of illumination and awakening; but at present we are still in the first stage of meditation: the old Adam must die, the immortal man remains to be conceived and born. Still deeper forces are now evoked and called to consciousness, and the path of transformation is undertaken. The Chinese believe that before entering on this path, a man should be around forty years of age. (Rousselle, 1960, p. 80)

The second stage is characterized by the practice of the

"backward flowing motion" in meditation. Energy is not permitted to disperse or flow outward through the activities of the lower centers. Instead, the energy is directed back inward and then upward along the kundalini pathway:

"In man, *logos* and *eros* (cognition and emotion), heart and kidneys are the great contradictory principles, equivalent to fire and water. The natural man allows both principles to flow out of him as thinking and begetting. But we must now gather them in, so that consciousness and the force of immortality may fructify one another. This turning back of energy, this temporary asceticism, is termed the "backward-flowing movement"; or it is described in the verse: "The river of heaven (the Milky Way) is flowing upstream." (Rousselle, 1960, p. 97)

The "Padme" is associated with the creative image and form. Rousselle's third stage shows a particularly close resemblance to this part of the mantra, even referring to the lotus:

The embryo is pressing to be born. Our immortal essence assumes the imaginary form of a *puer aeternus*, rises up, bursts through the skull in the region of the third eye, and with a shout that is echoed by the heavens, is born. The reborn man sits immortal on the lotus throne over our head. (Rousselle, 1960, p. 99)

Like the Buddhist "Hum", the fourth stage of Taoist meditation is enlightenment, as the infinite manifests in the finite. Having united in himself the polarities of his being, "man has become the universe: 'The whole world is contained in one grain'" (Rousselle, 1960, p. 83-84).

Evelyn Underhill and meditation. In her study of mysticism, Underhill describes the process leading to enlightenment. This process is demonstrated in the practice of introversion through its three stages:

1. Recollection is the first stage and, as mentioned in Chapter 3, is the most difficult stage, involving as it does an act of will to go against the habits and impulses of the mind.

2. The second stage is the experience of "Quiet" — a level of experience "for which human speech has few equivalents. . .characterized by an immense increase in the receptivity of the self, and by an almost complete suspension of the reflective powers" (Underhill, 1910, p. 317). In this stage, the struggle to concentrate is replaced by a "self-acting recollection." Many initially find this stage startling because of the absence of all accustomed mental workings.

The "Quiet" is potentially the most misleading to the spiritual seeker because its alert stillness can turn up the limp passivity that characterized the movement called "Quietism." This group has taken the peace and regeneration of this state to be the goal. Mystics who have understood that the Quiet is *not* an end in itself have also been the target of accusations that have been directed at the Quietists:

"Quiet" is the danger-zone of introversion. Of all forms of mystical activity, perhaps this has been the most abused, the least understood. Its theory, seized upon, divorced from its context, and developed to excess, produced the foolish and dangerous exaggerations of Quietism: and these, in their turn, caused a wholesale condemnation of the principle of passivity, and made many superficial persons regard "naked orison" as an essentially heretical act. The accusation of Quietism has been hurled at mystics whose only fault was a looseness of language which laid them open to misapprehension. (Underhill, 1910, p. 322)

Underhill describes Quietism as "absorption in nothing at all" with the purpose to "luxuriate in its peaceful effects" (1910, p. 322). She mentions the Transcendentalists as examples of this movement, leading to the possible conclusion that Transcendental Meditation (as taught in this country, but introduced long after Underhill's book was published) may lead its followers into the temptation and potential entrapment of this second stage:

Much of the teaching of modern "mystical" cults is thus crudely quietistic. It insists on the necessity of "going into the silence," and even, with a strange temerity, gives preparatory lessons in subconscious meditation: a proceeding which might well provoke the laughter of the saints. The faithful, being gathered together, are taught by simple exercises in recollection the way to attain the "Quiet." By this mental trick the modern transcendentalist naturally attains to a state of vacant placidity, in which he rests: and "remaining in a distracted idleness and misspending the time in expectation of extraordinary visits," believes — with a faith which many of the orthodox might envy — that he is here "united with his Principle." (Underhill, 1910, p. 324)

Contrast this with the understanding that the Quiet is a stage of *preparation*. It is only an opening of the door, and "That which comes in when the door is opened will be that which we truly and passionately desire" (Underhill, 1910, p. 324).

3. In the third stage, which Underhill called Contemplation, the self transcends the stillness of Quiet and is energized enthusiastically "on those high levels which are dark to the intellect but radiant to the heart" (Underhill, 1910, pp. 328-329). The greatest contemplatives have been able to sustain this third state for only the briefest of moments. Underhill defines two conditions that are present in this experience:

"Whatever terms he may employ to describe it, and however faint or confused his perceptions may be, the mystic's experience in Contemplation is the experience of the All, and this experience seems to him to be *given* rather than attained. . . .

This revealed Reality is apprehended by way of participation, not by way of observation. The passive receptivity of the Quiet is here developed into an active, outgoing self-donation, which is the self's response to the Divine initiative. (Underhill, 1910, p. 333)

* * *

In this chapter, we have identified an archetypal pattern

to which we aspire in our journey toward enlightenment. We have also pointed out the remarkable parallels between diverse Eastern and Western traditions in how meditation provides the essential vehicle for making that spiritual journey and achieving the realization of who we really are.

In the next chapter, we will look at the physical side of meditation — what happens in our bodies when we meditate.

Chapter 8
What Happens In Our Bodies When We Meditate

For hundreds of years, theology, philosophy, and psychology have been concerned about the nature of any connection between the infinite and the finite. If there is a soul, with its attributes of the infinite, how is it able to affect the finite, physical man? Several of our comparative sources suggest that the spiritual centers within the body provide a partial answer to this question. These centers (called chakras in Eastern writings) are often associated with seven endocrine glands and the energy fields related to each. Although there may be slight differences among various traditions concerning which endocrine glands are involved, Cayce and Stanford both use this configuration: gonads, cells of Leydig, adrenals, thymus, thyroid, pineal, and pituitary (see Figure 3).

Many psychics have described vortices of energy (invisible to most individuals) which touch at points in the physical body corresponding to the seven endocrine glands. One might compare this to magnetized iron that has a measurable energy field surrounding it. What we *see* is the iron;

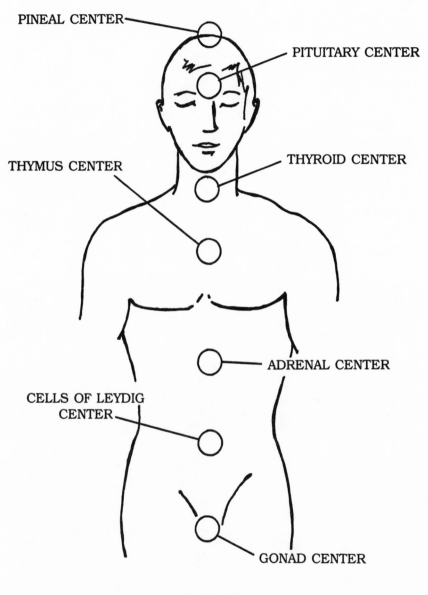

Figure 3
The body's endocrine glands
serving as spiritual centers

but the invisible energy pattern is essential to an understanding of the iron's properties.

The quality of these chakras (sometimes spelled "cakras") as contact points is described by Govinda:

In other words, these *cakras* are the points in which psychic forces and bodily functions merge into each other or penetrate each other. They are the focal points in which cosmic and psychic energies crystallize into bodily qualities, and in which bodily qualities are dissolved or transmuted again into psychic forces. "The seat of the soul is where the inner and outer world meet. When they penetrate each other, it is present in every point of penetration" (Novalis). We, therefore, can say that each psychic center in which we become conscious of this spiritual penetration, becomes the seat of the soul, and that by activating or awakening the activities of the various centers, we spiritualize and transform our body. (Govinda, 1969, p. 135)

In meditation, these centers may become more integrated with one another and more attuned to the Christ consciousness pattern. *The Secret of the Golden Flower* refers to this process by saying, "The seed-blossoms of the human body must be concentrated upward in the empty space" (Wilhelm, 1962, p. 33). This integration and attunement manifests in the physical as a change in the actual chemical activity of the body. In one research study, for example, meditators showed a significant decrease in the concentration of blood lactate, which has been correlated with the presence of anxiety (Wallace & Benson, 1973).

A word for the function of these spiritual centers is "transducer," defined as a device activated by power from one system and supplying power in another form to a second system. For the spiritual centers, the two systems referred to are the soul (with its access to the infinite supply of energy) and the energy we perceive as the physical man. Although no analogy is exact, the spiritual centers function somewhat like valves in that they regulate the flow of the one creative life force into the physical body.

Our work on earth is to integrate the activities of these centers. When we achieve this integration of energy fields, they are capable of transducing a higher vibrational energy that can manifest as healing in ourselves and others. In contrast, imbalance among these centers is likely to result in imbalanced experiences for an individual.

Activity at one of these spiritual contact points is sometimes referred to as "opening a center." To open these centers means to lessen the barrier between the finite and the infinite aspects of oneself — a goal of the spiritual seeker. The question is how to go about doing it.

The Cayce readings answer that question in information given to individuals studying *The Revelation of John.* These readings suggest that this New Testament book is a description of meditation experiences, and that the seven churches of Asia correspond to the seven spiritual centers of the body. At one point in *The Revelation,* John sees a book with seven seals on it. The Cayce source interprets the book as the body and the seven seals as those seven centers within the body (Cayce Reading 281-29). John cries out because he knows that no one in heaven or earth is worthy to open those seals. However, at that moment the Christ appears — the lamb — and opens them (Revelation 5). This symbology suggests an answer to most questions about the use of drugs, chants, or any technique that tries to manipulate the activities of these centers. The only force that should open them is the spirit of the Christ within. The *natural* response of the spiritual centers is to open as one seeks to apply the qualities of the Christ consciousness in one's daily life:

As has been experienced, this opening of the centers or the raising of the life force may be brought about by certain characters of breathing — for, as indicated, the breath is power in itself; and this power may be directed to certain portions of the body. But for what purpose? As yet it has been only to see what will happen! (Cayce Reading 2475-1)

The Cayce readings go on to say that the opening of the

spiritual centers can be directly related to the proper use of the Lord's Prayer:

> Q. Does the outline of the Lord's Prayer. . .have any bearing on the opening of the centers?
>
> A. Here is indicated the manner. . .the purpose for which it was given. (281-29)

The implication is that Jesus's purpose as He gave this prayer was to awaken an integrated activity of the spiritual centers. By stilling the mind and focusing the attention on the inner response to the words of the prayer, we begin to attune ourselves to the Christ archetype.

Before considering the individual characteristics of each of the seven spiritual centers, note three concepts found in the sources used for this book which deal with the physiology of meditation:

1. **All of the endocrine centers relate to one another.** Research in endocrinology provides extensive information describing how the ductless glands affect each other (Green, 1970, pp. 18-29; Easton, 1974, pp. 252-266). Considering meditation, this means we cannot describe accurately the activities of any one center in an individual without information concerning the activities of the other centers in that particular body.

2. **In meditation, the centers are awakened in a sequential order.** That order is physically from the lowest in the body to the highest, except in the case of the pituitary which is awakened last, although located slightly lower than the pineal (Stanford, 1977, p. 143). This sequential awakening is described as a movement of energy and is often referred to as the "kundalini pathway." Sources dealing with the Taoist approach refer to it as "the circulation of the light." The word "circulation" refers to the notion that this energy moves back down through the lower centers after having reached the pituitary. Only after reaching this highest center in the body does the energy attain the vibrational quality that can fulfill its potential to heal and to attune the activities of the centers to the Christ archetype.

3. **The centers can be grouped into three sections:** the lower three (gonads, cells of Leydig, and adrenals), the middle or heart center (thymus), and the upper three (thyroid, pineal, and pituitary). Such a division appears in many schools of meditation and puts particular emphasis on the heart center as the mediator between the upper and the lower groups. Examples of this grouping are found in Govinda and Rousselle:

> . . .according to Tibetan tradition, [the Centers] are divided into three zones: an upper one *(stod)*, to which the Centers of the brain and of the throat belong; a middle one *(bar)*, to which the Heart Center belongs; and a lower one *(smad)*, to which the solar plexus and the organs of reproduction belong. (Govinda, 1969, p. 173)

> . . .the "upper" field is in the middle of the forehead, seat of the "radiance of our essential nature" *(hsing kuang)*; the "middle" field is in the heart, the true source of the cinnabar-red elixir and of the conscious soul *(hun)*; and the "true" field is in the middle of the body (approximately from the navel to the kidneys), seat of the vital force *(ming)* and of the lower soul *(p'o)*. (Rousselle, 1960, p. 66-67)

Stanford's *The Spirit Unto the Churches* provides perhaps the most extensive description of the qualities and activities of the individual centers. Following are some major points for each center:

Gonads

The gonads (testes in the male and ovaries in the female) are the transformer and condenser of the one energy as it is expressed in the body. That basic energy is not sexual, although it can be expressed in that way. Freudian psychology is relevant to the extent that we see ourselves merely as physical beings. When we identify with the material, finite nature of our being, and ignore the spiritual dimension, the activities of the cells of Leydig, adrenals, and thymus revolve about the gonads, which are often symbolized by the earth.

The following passage summarizes how the energy of the gonads is drawn upon and used by the other centers:

When there is the release of this force in a sexual climax, it is released in a relationship more directly to the cells of Leydig (although affecting other centers, too). When it is expressed in determination to get something done, or in anger, or in fear — particularly fear at the physical plane, or defensive fear in the more external sense — it relates to the adrenal center. When it relates to compassion, to love (as in the relationship of oneness, help, and the extending out of oneself in a mother to a child), or to the feeling and the sense of well-being, it manifests through the heart or thymus center.

However, when this sexual force manifests as speech — as ecstatic speech (speaking in ecstasy or in tongues), as dissertation through the voice, as the use of the voice in various ways, destructively or constructively — it manifests through the will or throat center. When it manifests through the intellect, the brilliance of mind and thought, it operates by a major part through the pineal gland. When in meditation, in the ecstasy of God-consciousness and peace and stillness and love in its highest form, this gonadal energy is being directed, manifesting through, and returning downward to transform from the pituitary center. Thus, the difference should be clear. (Stanford, 1977, pp. 14-15)

Govinda's description of the gonadal center makes clear the possibility of aligning or attaining it with the activities of the higher centers, thereby using this energy as an aid to awakening spiritual consciousness:

The lowest of these centers, which represents the Element Earth, is called *Mūlādhāra-Cakra* ("Root-support"), and is situated at the base of the spinal column. It corresponds to the *plexus pelvis* in Western physiology and contains the still unqualified, primordial vital energy, which serves either the functions of physical reproduction and rejuvenation or brings about the sublimation of these forces into spiritual potentialities.

The latent energy of this center is depicted as the dormant force of the goddess *Kundalini* — who as the *śakti* of *Brahma* embodies the potentiality of nature, whose effects may be either divine or demoniacal. The wise, who control these forces, may reach through them the highest spiritual power and perfection, while those who ignorantly release them, will be destroyed by them. (Govinda, 1969, p. 139)

In Stanford's readings, *conscious purposefulness* is the transforming element for the activities of the gonads. Through devotion, service, and discernment (the capacity to differentiate between what leads to higher awareness and what does not), the gonads help us move forward in our efforts to achieve awareness of the infinite in the finite.

Cells of Leydig

The cells of Leydig are located within the testes or ovaries and within the adrenals. Water is the most frequent symbol for this center. In sexual climax, the cells of Leydig draw upon the gonads, resulting in the movement of energy through this center, but in an *outward* direction. The energy moving through this center may be perceived incorrectly as a movement *upward*, such as is experienced in meditation. Here then is our temptation: will we use the energies of our bodies to awaken faculties of higher consciousness or to express ourselves *merely* in terms of our physical nature? No other human activity presents such a clear choice as does the sex drive. Will we bring a consciously chosen spiritual ideal into our sexual activity, or will we attend only to the physical sensations of sexual release? This question has been debated for centuries by those seeking higher states of awareness. Because the cells of Leydig are so closely related to the endocrine processes of sexual expression and to the development of the secondary sex characteristics (e.g., voice changes, hair growth patterns), they are usually associated with the concept of temptation in studies of the spiritual centers.

Adrenals

The adrenal center (or solar plexus center) is referred to as the "god of the earth" because it is easily awakened by patterns developed within the finite earthly boundaries we perceive as our limits. This center is the *distributor* of energies in response to the will. So if the will is directed towards a limited identity of ourselves (i.e., our physical-consciousness egos), the expressions of this center can include stubbornness, resentment, and anger. Our "fight or flight" instinct is activated through this center by the release of adrenaline into the blood stream. The qualities of personality affected by this center are described by Stanford in the following passage:

As to negative emotions or attitudes expressed that come through the adrenal center: pride, in part, in one of its aspects; particularly anger, where it hates others, where it makes the mind unconscious of its source; hatred; despise and jealousy. Jealousy is closely related, of course, to the gonad and Leydig centers, but it manifests more through the adrenal center, for jealousy is a fire that burns within. The expression of these emotions or attitudes, in not being conscious of how they make a person operate in body and mind, in his or her own consciousness, is in itself sinful or destructive, once one is conscious of the forces involved.

As to positive attitudes, the ability to laugh comes in a great part through the adrenal center—to laugh in the presence of circumstance, where it is needed or helpful to the mind. To persist, to continue, in the presence of difficulty is also a positive expression of the adrenal. To observe another's weakness and not get angry, but rather to uplift another and be willing to help is to bring the influence of the heart center (the air center) and the adrenal (the fire center) into

a proper relationship. To manifest strength of purpose
of any kind, if the purpose is good, is a positive expression of the adrenal center. (Stanford, 1977, pp. 50-51)

The adrenal center is frequently symbolized by fire or by
the lion (or any of the great cats). It is often related to
psychism and particularly with mediumship:

That is why so many who have the adrenal type of
psychism become mediums. For it is this center that
can exude so much astral energy and can feed the
unregenerate spirits and the astral bodies of beings
that are seeking energy. The adrenal center is particularly receptive to astral influence, because it is that
center which combines the subtle, the air, into the
solid in a fire—an astral fire. (Stanford, 1977, p. 56)

Perhaps Stanford's most important point in his description of this center concerns our preoccupation with speed
and our lack of interest in turning this energy *upward* in
meditation to awaken a higher state of consciousness.
Stanford attributes this to our fear of the responsibility
that comes in recognizing our inner, spiritual nature. Expressions of speed and power represent the use of energy
at an adrenal level that is directed *outward* instead of *upward*. Referring to the symbol of the great cat for the adrenals he cites two advertising slogans popular in the early
1970's as characteristic of our culture's overconcern for this
center: "Put a tiger in your tank," and "Get the tiger's paws
for your car" (1977, Stanford, p. 59).

Thymus

The thymus center (or heart center) is the arbitrator between the lower three centers and the upper three. From
the activities of this center, we begin to identify ourselves
with the qualities of our spiritual nature as represented in
the thyroid, pineal, and pituitary. This "change of heart" is
shaped by the *affinities* we have with the world around us.
Affinity or "love" (in the broadest sense of the word) encom-
passes every experience we have where we communicate
with someone or have a feeling for something outside of

ourselves. This love and "recognition of the other" is always related to the thymus center. The following passage summarizes how the thymus can serve through love to unite the activities of the lower and upper centers:

What is seen in the very nature of man in his complexity? The seeming opposites of the spiritual and the physical. We have the God of heavens and the god of the earth. We have between them, in a sense, the arbitrator—the thymus. "Thy kingdom come, thy will be done in earth as it is in heaven"—through love. Love is that which makes whole or recognizes the wholeness, the oneness of the lower with the higher. Hence, wherever there is love expressed at any level from one person to another, dispersed from a person or within a person, we see an influence upon the thymus. (Stanford, 1977, p. 80)

When the thymus fails to operate in such an integrative way, its activities manifest as grief, emotional depression, and self-pity. In its positive function, the thymus helps keep the body free from disease through its influence upon the white blood cells.

The thymus center is frequently symbolized by the eagle (or another bird) or by the air. Because of its location near the lungs, its activity is often depicted in dreams by the wind, tornados, objects being thrown through the air, or various aircraft. Reflecting its nature as the mediator, it can also be symbolized by functions requiring balance, such as a tightrope walker or a juggler.

Perhaps the most noticeable quality of an individual in whom the thymus is working in an integrative fashion is the absence of fear. Stanford's description points to important relations between this center and the adrenals and the pituitary:

Hence, where there comes perfect love, there can be no fear. Why? Fear comes about by an attitude of mind consciousness, but at the physical level there is immediately that excitation of the adrenal. The heart starts beating faster. How does this relate to the thymus? The very same hormones that stimulate the increased activity of the heart and blood circulation stimulate the thymus at the same time. They will stimulate it in several different ways: in its ability to produce parent cells for immunological purposes; in its relationship to changes in the control of cell integrity in the body; in its relationship to the circulatory and the lymphatic systems; and in many other ways. But the same hormones are responsible.

However, where the love is perfect, where there is a perfect balance in the thymus, it responds perfectly to the signal from the pituitary. Therefore, by its reaction and its hormones upon the adrenal itself, as well as by the strength of its own impulse, it cannot be fully affected by any—even inadvertent—impulses from the adrenal. So, the person cannot fear at the physical level, and will not fear. (Stanford, 1977, p. 82)

Thyroid

The thyroid center (or throat center) is most often associated with the human will. This soul faculty is a complex topic and must be seen in a far broader context than merely choice. In fact, much of what we call will-directed choice isn't that at all. Instead, we can see upon honest self-observation that mental patterns (often subconscious) which are linked to one of the four lower centers often compel us to decisions with little or no real freedom.

Will is a part of the Godhead within us and directs us toward the expression of the infinite in the finite. This higher will is not reached by an intellectual process. We cannot determine through logic the will of the Godhead within us. Only through devotion and purposefulness do we become conscious of that higher will being expressed in the finite. As discussed earlier, meditation is not a logical, rational process of the mind. This point rests largely upon understanding the qualities of the thyroid center. The spiritual search is not so much an effort of the earthly forces to reach up and establish a place for themselves among the infinite forces (recall the story of the Tower of Babel and the confusion at the throat or speech level); instead, our search is the effort of the infinite forces to descend into a receptive and sincere finite expression.

Qualities related to an imbalance in this center include stubbornness and not listening to others. The phrase "a stiff-necked people" refers to activities of this center. Because of the proximity of the throat to those structures which produce speech and sound, the voice can play a role in attunement of this center:

> The use of chants in devotions are important in attuning the will toward a higher manifestation. The reason for this is that when a chant is used, whether it is that called a mantra or any type chanted for spiritual purposes of devotion, the heart is filled with something other than those things which gratify the bodily consciousness. And there is only one direction from which this can come—from above. It is always exerted and controlled by the thyroid, the will center, that in which the Word is manifested by seeking devotion (which is an aspect of the heart center) and by using the voice, the throat, musically. (Stanford, 1977, p. 106)

The thyroid is most often symbolized by images related to the throat area, to speech, or to words (e.g., the neck, the tongue, a hangman's noose, a book).

Pineal

The pineal center (or crown center) has often been referred to as the third eye, although some systems prefer to associate the pituitary center with the third eye. This center is the major influence to the mind, and to the intellect in particular. As this center is awakened in us, we have access to all knowledge and to memory of all past experiences. Its activity, especially in meditation, is closely related to the cells of Leydig. The following passage describes that relationship and several factors related to correctly awakening the energies of the spiritual centers. Of particular importance is the difference between conditions producing emotional or psychic disturbances and conditions producing integrative meditation experiences:

There is a special impulse from the pineal at a physical level and at a hormonal level that relates especially to the Leydig. There is a special impulse that can come from the pineal in response to consciousness, that can cause a rising up of an energy from the gonad forces through the agency of the Leydig. In an ultimate sense, this energy moves through a more central portion of the spine. Normally it is imbalanced and dispersed into the activities of the world through the two channels upon either side of the spine and the nerves (the "ida" and "pingala," in yogic terminology). However, in the presence of this special impulse, this energy rises and passes as an impulse through the *central channels* of the spine. It moves upward, reaching the level of the pineal, in response to that which first came from above.

Now, understand this. It is an important point. Many persons inadvertently or by false dedication, seeking psychic phenomena or other things, awaken by certain means an aspect of this gonadal energy through an inadvertent condition of the Leydig *without* the calling up from above, from the pineal. When this happens, the energy frequently becomes dispersed at various glandular levels upon the way and may create all manner of emotional or physical disturbances, which are seen as spontaneous manifestations of what could be called emotional, mental, or psychical disturbances. (Stanford, 1977, pp. 142-143)

These Stanford readings go on to describe the relationship between the pineal and the cells of Leydig, referring to a hormonal key that awakens the cells of Leydig. The following is perhaps the most important passage in the Stanford readings concerning the process of meditation:

There is the key in the pineal center to unlock the door of the body, and indeed to unlock the door to the kingdom of heaven. See, it depends on which way you are going. Look, some have misinterpreted and said that the pineal is the door. It is not the door. The *Leydig* is the door. The pineal is the key of the kingdom of heaven and *to* the kingdom of heaven. The key is sent down, at a physical level and a hormone level and a mind level, from the pineal to activate the Leydig center in a very certain way. At this point the Leydig is so stabilized and channeled, or opened as a door, that the temptation forces, the mind forces, the imaginative forces are stilled and stabilized by a singular impulse of energy exchange between the lower centers and the higher.

Understand, the key is not of this world. It is the key of and to the kingdom of heaven. It can unlock the earth or open it to the heavens. (Stanford, 1977, p. 147)

Pituitary

The pituitary gland (or brow center) is the master gland of the body. As this center is awakened, there comes the awareness of the *oneness* of all being. Its primary quality is service, which Stanford defines as "a state of enlightenment when the finite consciousness of man enters the light" (Stanford, 1977, p. 175).

Once the energy awakened in meditation reaches the pineal (as described above), it builds up to the point where it passes across to the pituitary, bringing into awareness the qualities of consciousness related to that highest center. Those qualities are divine love, service, and a sense of oneness. The passage of energy from the pineal to the pituitary stimulates the optic nerve and creates the sensation of a blinding light (for some, such as St. Paul, "blinding" is at least temporarily a literal fact).

The Secret of the Golden Flower refers to the pituitary as the heavenly heart. The second passage below makes reference as well to the earthly heart, which can be interpreted as the thymus center under the influence of the three lower centers:

The work on the circulation of the light depends entirely on the backward-flowing movement, so that the thoughts (the place of heavenly consciousness, the heavenly heart) are gathered together. The heavenly heart lies between the sun and the moon (i.e., between the two eyes).

The *Book of the Yellow Castle* says: "In the square inch field of the square foot house, life can be regulated." The square foot house is the face. The square inch field in the face: what could that be other than the heavenly heart? (Wilhelm, 1962, p. 22)

When men are set free from the womb, the primal spirit dwells in the square inch (between the eyes), but the conscious spirit dwells below in the heart. This lower fleshly heart has the shape of a large peach: it is covered by the wings of the lungs, supported by the liver, and served by the bowels. This heart is dependent on the outside world.

The lower heart moves like a strong, powerful commander who despises the heavenly ruler because of his weakness, and has usurped the leadership in affairs of state. But when the primal castle can be fortified and defended, then it is as if a strong and wise ruler sat upon the throne. (Wilhelm, 1962, p. 25)

The circulation of the light is completed as the energy passes back to the other centers, this time imparting the vibrational qualities taken on by its contact with the pituitary. That vibration can best be described as healing, for it stimulates an integrative functioning of each of the spiritual centers. This is the physiological goal of meditation.

According to Govinda, an understanding of the nature of the spiritual centers gives us insight into the nature of the universe. The human being is a microcosmic representation of the macrocosm:

The seven Centers of the human body represent in a certain way the elementary structure and dimensionality of the universe: from the state of greatest density and materiality up to the state of immaterial multi-dimensional extension; from the organs of dark, subconscious, but cosmically powerful primoridal forces to those of a radiant, enlightened consciousness. That the form-potentialities of the whole universe are latent in these centers, is hinted at by attributing to them all the sounds of the Sanskrit alphabet in the form of seed-syllables. (Govinda, 1969, p. 142)

What more fitting way to conclude the discussion of the physical side of meditation than by seeing ourselves as representations of the universe in miniature!

Chapter 9
How East Meets West
In Meditation Tradition

Throughout this book, we have read and analyzed many passages on meditation from *The Secret of the Golden Flower* and the writings of Lama Govinda. Together with the paper by Rousselle, these sources have well represented two of the Eastern spiritual traditions — Chinese Taoism and Tibetan Buddhism. For many years in the United States, meditation was considered by many only as an import from the East, and therefore alien and perhaps even sinister in its presence here.

Yet, side by side with those Eastern writings, we have in this book, looked at passages representing the Western traditions, especially those of Christian mysticism summarized by Underhill and Heiler, the scientific approach of Naranjo and Ornstein, the psychological foundation laid by Jung, and the intuitive sources recorded through Cayce and Stanford, both of Western tradition background. That Western foundation seems much less known or acknowledged by those who would label meditation as primarily an imported Eastern religious practice.

Several specific aspects of meditation — for example, the use of mantras or affirmations, the control of breathing, and the specific location of spiritual centers — differ among various traditions. However, a closer look would demonstrate that these differences are as great among some Eastern traditions as they are between Eastern and Western approaches.

More evident is the strong common foundation in all these traditions for the practice of some form of meditation and, beyond that, for the philosophy of the nature of humanity and the reasons for our physical existence. This leads to the conclusion that we need not look to the East for either a rationale or a technique for our meditation. In fact, there may be strong reasons for Westerners *not* to adopt some of the Eastern approaches to meditation.

Jung, for example, warns against the adoption by Westerners of Eastern techniques and teachings (1962, pp. 83-85). The danger is that, in such an adoption, we will throw away our Western heritage and find ourselves with Eastern traditions not suited to the psychic evolution we have experienced. The intellect has been highly developed in Europe and America, but the insights of Chinese philosophy come from the intuitive function. Rather than impose intellect upon these teachings, Jung suggests that Westerners (e.g., Europeans in the following passage) would do better to develop their own inner nature and thereby surpass the developments of the East:

If we would succeed in elevating another, or even a third psychic function to the dignity accorded intellect, then the West might expect to surpass the East by a very great margin. Therefore it is sad indeed when the European departs from his own nature and imitates the East or "affects" it in any way. The possibilities open to him would be so much greater if he would remain true to himself and develop out of his own nature all that the East has brought forth from its inner being in the course of the centuries. (Jung, 1962, pp. 85-86)

One way this can be done is through an exploration of the unconscious. The West has not trusted fantasy, labeling it subjective daydreaming, while the East abounds in images and symbols related to the spiritual quest. They long ago extracted the essence of images arising from the unconscious and condensed it into spiritual teachings. Jung feels strongly that the Westerner must now begin to experience fantasy and find "the sense in apparent nonsense" (1962, p. 120). This is *not* an invitation to daydream in *meditation*. Instead, it would provide us with the opportunity to experience, through dreams and reverie, a forgotten part of ourselves. Meditation, as it has been described, would act as a selective agent, attuning an individual so that the unconscious content allowed to awaken in fantasy will lead to greater integration and psychic balance. In doing this, the West may reach deeper insights than those of the East:

> We may rest assured that what we extract from our experiences will differ from what the East offers us today. The East came to its knowledge of inner things in relative ignorance of the external world. We, on the other hand, will investigate the psyche and its depths supported by a tremendously extensive historical and scientific knowledge. (Jung, 1962, pp. 120-121)

Heiler supports the notion that we in the West need not look to the East to find guidance concerning meditation. He admits that the contemplative tradition has been buried and is unknown to most modern-day Christians:

> The exaggerated dynamism of the concept of God that recognizes only a "Deus semper actuosus et numquam otiosus," a God always active and never idle, and the related hostility to the static Platonic conception of God, have given rise to a highly anticontemplative attitude. Nevertheless, the contemplative attitude is not entirely lacking, but has merely been submerged. It cannot die as long as the Old and New Testaments continue to be generally accepted. (Heiler, 1960, p. 201)

He goes on to say that Christian mysticism overshadows

non-Christian mysticism by its scope, its richness, and its diversity. He agrees that the study of non-Christian forms of meditation *can* provide valuable stimulus and suggestions, yet asserts that those sources hold nothing entirely new for one who has thoroughly studied Western mysticism. He sees the modern-day attraction to Eastern philosophy as a reaction to the unavailability of parallel knowledge from the Western tradition. In his study of that tradition, Heiler names Plato and Plotinus as the great teachers of Christian mystics. Philo took the first decisive step in his treatise *On the Contemplative Life* to synthesize the prophetic tradition of the Old Testament with elements of mysticism:

> This fusion of Biblical-prophetic piety and of Platonic-Neoplatonic mysticism is the most grandiose synthesis of diverse religious forms known to the history of religion, greater even than the memorable synthesis of old Islamic religion and Gnostic-Neoplatonic-Indian mysticism that occurred in Sūfism. (Heiler, 1960, p. 194)

After this, Heiler credits Clement and Origen with the synthesis of Biblical Christianity and Platonism. And finally, Neoplatonism influenced Christianity through Dionysus the Areopagite, a mysterious figure criticized by many modern Protestants. Heiler describes the work of the Areopagite in this way:

> For him God is the "inaccessible light". . .that can be seen only in a "nonseeing" that transcends all sensory perception and intellection. . . .In this nonseeing, imageless vision lies for him the secret of the. . .mystical contemplation. (Heiler, 1960, p. 196)

        ★ ★ ★

All this supports the proposition that the practice of meditation and its inner power of silence, such as has been presented in this book, is relevant to our culture — especially in a "universal" form as described. Not only is it a part of our heritage (no matter how forgotten), but the West may have the opportunity to experience insights into human nature even deeper than those from the East. Regardless of the sources used to define this integrated, universal approach — coming as they do from many cultures and historical periods — they all point to meditation as an essential and powerful activity in our unending search for fulfillment and self-realization.

Appendix
What Science Says About Meditation

The years since 1970 have seen a major growth in the number of scientific research studies focusing on meditation. As the practice of meditation has become more widespread in the West, so has the West's interest in objectively validating the subjective effects reported by meditators.

Meditation research studies can be divided into several areas: the physiology of meditation, techniques of meditation, psychological effects, parapsychological effects, behavioral effects, group and social effects, and general effects. This chapter is not a definitive survey of such research, but illustrates each of these research areas with examples of interesting studies and results. To represent the complete range of research, included are examples of studies without supporting results.

Research on the Physiology of Meditation
One of the classical studies in this area was done by Wallace and Benson with subjects practicing transcendental meditation. They describe this state as a "wakeful,

hypometabolic" state with the following characteristics:

There is a reduction in oxygen consumption, carbon dioxide elimination and the rate and volume of respiration; a slight increase in the acidity of the arterial blood; a marked decrease in the blood-lactate level; a slowing of the heartbeat; a considerable increase in skin resistence; and an electroencephalogram pattern of intensification of slow alpha waves with occasional theta-wave activity. (Wallace & Benson, 1973, p. 266)

Of particular interest is the decrease in the lactate concentration in the blood (an indication of metabolism in the absence of free oxygen). They found that during the first 10 minutes of meditation, the concentration decreased nearly four times faster than the rate of decrease in people normally resting in the supine position. They quote previous studies that have shown that patients with anxiety neurosis show a large rise in blood lactate when they are placed under stress.

Benson has continued not only to undertake research on the meditation process and specifically on the "non-cultic" technique he refers to as the "relaxation response," but also to publish books which have contributed to a popular surge of interest in the process (e.g., Benson, 1975). In one of his most interesting studies, Benson and associates found that Tibetan Buddhist advanced meditators, investigated with the help of the Dalai Lama, were able to increase the temperature of their fingers and toes by as much as 8.3 degrees Centigrade (Benson et al, 1982).

Wallace and his associates published a study reporting that long-term meditators exhibited physiological and perceptual capacities of people 12 years younger than their actual chronological age (Wallace et al, 1982). The specific differences were in auditory thresholds, close-up vision, and blood pressure.

Studying both short- and long-range effects of meditation on the neuromuscular system, Warshal (1980) suggests that meditation may result in shorter reflex times, possibly because of a heightened sensitivity of the human nervous system.

One result emerging from the Benson research as well as from other studies is that same physiological responses to meditation — as measured in terms of such common indicators as galvanic skin response, blood pressure, respiratory rate, pulse rate, or electroencephalogram (EEG) — are not unique to meditation, but may occur with other simpler relaxation techniques, including "just sitting." Shapiro (1982) has provided probably the most comprehensive summary and comparison to date of the physiological effects of meditation " and other self-control strategies." His overview includes 83 references on meditation and he cites four previous major reviews of the meditation literature.

However, no research has been identified where the physiological activity at the endocrine centers during meditation has been studied. Research on the pineal gland by Dr. Richard Wurtman and his associates at the Massachusetts Institute of Technology, for example, suggests still-undeciphered functions for this gland Descartes called the seat of the rational soul (Schmeck, 1984). As presented in Chapter 8, the activity at the spiritual centers is the critical connection between the infinite and the finite, and everything else physiologically pales by comparison. But as yet, traditional science has not produced research support for this philosophy.

Research on Techniques of Meditation

In research on a home-study approach to learning and practicing meditation, Puryear, Cayce, and Thurston (1976) found a significant reduction in anxiety as measured by a psychological scale among those using a new workbook manual over those using their customary meditation techniques. (The approach in the manual had many of the features incorporated into the steps outlined in Chapter 3 of this book.)

The need for a special mantra during meditation has been explored by many researchers, and Delmonte (1983) reviews many of those studies to conclude that, like Benson's view, any mental device on which one can focus attention is as effective as any other in bringing about the *physiological* changes associated with meditation (see section above). Therefore, we can conclude that the choice of a focusing device is up to the meditator. Chapter 3 recommends focusing on an affirmation related to the ideal, because of its value in reaching toward the desired pattern of Christ consciousness, something beyond just the beneficial physical effects.

The value of the head and neck exercise in preparing for meditation, as recommended in Chapter 3, has been indirectly confirmed by the research of Dr. Donald Peterson of the Loma Linda University School of Medicine (Peterson, 1984). Peterson's research emphasizes specifically the value of these exercises in the relief of chronic headaches.

In support of the need to be patient in the early stages of meditation practice, Compton and Becker (1983) demonstrated that a learning period of about one year is normal in Zen meditation and that expectations for positive effects early in that period are unrealistic, accounting for some of the nonresults of studies with novice meditators.

Research on Psychological Effects of Meditation

Setting aside whether chronic pain is physiological or psychological, Kabat-Zinn demonstrated in a two-year study that sufferers of chronic pain for whom medical treatments had failed could learn to control pain through a meditation process (Kabat-Zinn, 1982). Similarly, Charlesworth (1984) taught groups of workers to monitor their blood pressure and, through techniques including progressive relaxation, deep breathing, imagery work, and autogenic methods, he helped them reduce their blood pressure levels significantly. Another study of workers in a telephone company (Carrington et al, 1980) demonstrated significant stress reduction as a result of worker training and practice of a meditation-relaxation technique. Of three techniques compared, the two that involved meditation had greater effects than the one that was primarily progressive relaxation.

In an extensive review of meditation research, West reports several studies with positive psychological effects from meditative practice (West, 1980). For example, a decrease in anxiety associated with meditation may also be accompanied by a decrease in neurotic tendencies. His summary also reinforces results mentioned above: In seven studies, for example, meditation was an effective means for controlling blood pressure, and insomnia and headaches have been successfully treated with meditation.

At Harvard Medical School, Brown (1983) and his associates have reported that long-term meditators may undergo major changes in their perceptual/cognitive states. They appear to have more refined mental control, greater discriminative capacities, and less emotional involvement with their thoughts. In a New Zealand study, Throll (1981) also demonstrated significant changes on personality measures in favorable directions by meditators, somewhat greater than those practicing progressive relaxation.

Research on Parapsychological Effects of Meditation

At least two studies point to an increase in psychic sensitivity by those who meditate. Schmeidler (1970) used six graduate students who called a set of cards at the beginning of the experimental session, underwent a brief session of breathing and meditation instruction by an Indian swami, then called another set of cards. Five of the six subjects had a significantly higher calling score after the meditation instruction. Osis (1971) reports a study designed to determine the dimensions of the meditation experience. Subjects' responses to questionnaire items immediately after each meditation period were factor analyzed. ESP tests were also given after meditation periods. Osis found that the factors of "self-transcendence" and "openness" were associated with positive ESP results.

In a study at the University of Ottawa, psychologists Busby and De Konick (1980) measured not only the personality changes resulting from meditation and relaxation exercises, but also recorded the effects those changes had on the meditators' dreams. Results showed a significant increase in fantasy elements and in instances of misfortune transformed into good fortune, and a decrease in aggressive dream mood. In another study of meditators' dreaming, Faber (1979) found that meditators recalled significantly more dreams than non-meditators, and that the dreams of meditators had more universal or archetypal content than those of nonmeditators. Specifically, the meditators' dreams were higher in mythological parallel, emotion, remoteness from everyday life, and irrationality — all signs of archetypality, according to Carl Jung.

Research on Behavioral Effects of Meditation

In this category are studies of the external behavior of people who meditate. For example, Fiebert and Mead (1981) looked for effects on academic performance of students who meditated. Their results indicate that students who meditated just prior to studying or taking exams achieved significantly higher grades than those who meditated at other times. Furthermore, all meditators spent less time studying without a drop in academic performance.

In a study of creative group problem solving, Kindler (1979) found that a group which meditated just before working on a problem took less time solving the problem, required fewer transactions among group members, felt calmer during the activity, and reported a greater sense of teamwork than a group which did not meditate. In another study of creativity, Travis (1980) found that meditators may increase their creativity in visual arts, but not their verbal creativity.

Wong and associates report that consistent meditation practice among a group of people dependent on drugs or alcohol was accompanied by a decrease of substance abuse, as long as they continued meditating (Wong et al, 1981). On various measures, the meditators also appeared less paranoic, less psychically debilitated, more satisfied and self-aware, and better able to achieve muscle relaxation.

Finally, research by the Arons showed that, of the women they studied, those who continued regular meditation for at least two years also had a higher level of marital adjustment than less regular and less experienced meditators (Aron and Aron, 1982). These researchers emphasize that this evidence of correlation does not necessarily indicate a cause-and-effect relationship between meditation and adjustment, but simply that they appeared together. This same reasoning is true of other studies where the results are based on correlation techniques, rather than on more experimental treatments.

Research on Group and Social Effects of Meditation

In addition to research on the effects of meditation on the consciousness of the individual meditator, some studies have attempted to assess the effects of meditation on mass consciousness — on society, as it were. The Arons, for example, conducted an experiment in Atlanta, Georgia, involving a group of meditators who meditated for an hour each night for six nights in a high-crime neighborhood (Aron and Aron, 1981). During this week, and the week immediately following, the incidence of violent crime fell dramatically in that district. The experiment was repeated on two other occasions with similar results — a drop of from 18 to 30% in violent crime. Comparable results have also been noted in an area surrounding a university with an estimated 1600 daily meditators (*The Daily Tribune*, 1982).

Research on the General Effects of Meditation

Since meditation — and many other relaxation techniques — appear to have so many positive effects on the individual, some research has been directed at seeing how far its effects would spread. For example, Hewitt and Miller (1981) tried to find out if meditators would generally enjoy other people more than non-meditators, but the results were not significant.

Several researchers have challenged the uniqueness of meditation, pointing to the many studies in which simple rest and relaxation techniques achieved many of the same results attributed to meditation. The most extensive scholarly analysis is that of Holmes (1984), with subsequent comments and counter-comments by Suler, West, Shapiro, Benson, Friedman, and Holmes (1985). The strongest criticism leveled at meditation in the most detracting of the studies seems to be that, with the objective measurements made thus far, meditation has effects which may be little different from the effects of resting.

As noted earlier, research has apparently not been done on the physiology of the endocrine system — the spiritual centers — during meditation, so science cannot comment yet on that critical phase of the meditation process. Similarly, science has not examined other spiritual aspects of meditation — and may not be able to with its current repertoire of measurement techniques.

However, research on meditation as a vehicle for enhancing one's spiritual development continues at the Association for Research and Enlightenment as part of its ongoing commitment to research (e.g., Puryear, Cayce, and Thurston, 1976; Kohr, 1976; and Sparrow, 1981). Until such a time as more spiritually-oriented research results are available, it remains for each individual to carry out a personal program of experimentation and self-evaluation on the more subtle, spiritual benefits of meditation. In the meantime, the consistently positive kinds of results summarized in this chapter and in the many other studies that could not be included here should be encouraging to the meditator — reason enough to seek the inner power of silence.

LIST OF REFERENCES

ARON, ELAINE N., and ARTHUR ARON. "Transcendental Meditation Program and Marital Adjustment," *Psychological Reports*, 1982, 51, pp. 887-890.

ARON, ELAINE N., and ARTHUR ARON. *Leading Edge*, February 2, 1981. [Article about meditation and crime control in Atlanta, reported in *Perspective on Consciousness and Psi Research*, 1981, 3(1), p.1; also follow-up study reported in *Perspective*, 1981, 3(7), p. 4.]

BENSON, HERBERT. *The Relaxation Response*. New York: William Morrow, 1975.

BENSON, HERBERT; JOHN W. LEHMANN; M. S. MALHOTRA; RALPH F. GOLDMAN; JEFFREY HOPKINS; and MARK D. EPSTEIN. "Body Temperature Changes During the Practice of g Tum-mo Yoga," *Nature*, 1982, 295, pp. 234-236.

BROWN, DANIEL; JACK ENGLER; and MICHAEL FORTE. "New Study: Meditators Show Refined Perception, Less Emotional Attachment," *Brain Mind Bulletin*, 1983,

8(7), pp. 1-2.

BUCKE, R. *Cosmic Consciousness.* New York: Dutton, 1901.

BUSBY, KEITH, and JOSEPH DE KONINCK. *Perceptual and Motor Skills,* 1980, 50. (Article about meditation and personality change, reported in *Perspective on Consciousness and Psi Research,* 1980, 2(4), pp. 1, 4.)

CARRINGTON, PATRICIA; GILBEART H. COLLINGS, JR.; HERBERT BENSON; HARRY ROBINSON; LORING W. WOOD; PAUL M. LEHRER; ROBERT L. WOOLFOLK; and JEAN W. COLE. "The Use of Meditation-Relaxation Techniques for the Management of Stress in a Working Population," *Journal of Occupational Medicine,* 1980, 22(4), pp. 221-231.

CAYCE, EDGAR. Unpublished readings, copyrighted by the Edgar Cayce Foundation, Virginia Beach, Virginia, 1945.

CHARLESWORTH, EDWARD A.; et al. "Stress Management at the Worksite for Hypertension: Compliance, Cost-Benefit, Health Care, and Hypertension-Related Variables," *Psychosomatic Medicine,* 1984, 46(5), pp. 387-397.

COMPTON, WILLIAM, and GORDON BECKER. *Journal of Clinical Psychology,* 1983, 39(6). [Article about learning period in Zen meditation, reported in *Perspective on Consciousness and Psi Research,* 1984, 5(12), pp. 1, 4.]

The Daily Tribune (Royal Oak, MI), November 13, 1982. [Article about meditation and crime control, reported in *Perspective on Consciousness and Psi Research,* 1983, 4(10), p. 3.]

DELMONTE, M. M. "Mantras and Meditation: A Literature Review," *Perceptual and Motor Skills,* 1983, 57, pp. 64-66.

EASTON, DEXTER. *Mechanisms of Body Functions.* Englewood Cliffs, NJ: Prentice-Hall, 1974.

FABER, PHILLIP. "Meditation and Archetypal Content of Nocturnal Dreams," *Journal of Analytical Psychology,* 23(1). [Reported in *Perspective on Consciousness and Psi Research,* 1979, 1(1), pp. 1-2.]

FIEBERT, MARTIN S. and TRAVIS M. MEAD. "Meditation and Academic Performance," *Perceptual and Motor Skills,* 1981, 53, pp. 447-450.

GREENE, RAYMOND. *Human Hormones.* New York: McGraw-Hill, 1970.

GOVINDA, LAMA ANAGARIKA. *Foundations of Tibetan Mysticism.* New York: Samuel Weiser, 1969.

GOVINDA, LAMA ANAGARIKA. *Creative Meditation and Multi-Dimensional Consciousness.* Wheaton, IL: Theosophical Publishing House, 1976.

HEILER, FRIEDRICH. "Contemplation in Christian Mysticism," in J. Campbell (Ed.), *Papers from the Eranos Yearbooks. Vol. 4: Spiritual Disciplines.* Princeton, NJ: Princeton University Press, 1960, pp. 186-238.

HEWITT, JAY, and RALPH MILLER. *Psychological Reports,* 1981, 48, 395-398. [Article about effects of meditation on enjoyment of others, reported in *Perspective on Consciosness and Psi Research,* 1981, 3(6), pp. 1-2.]

HOLMES, DAVID S. "Meditation and Somatic Arousal Reduction: A Review of the Experimental Evidence," *American Psychologist,* 1984, 39(1), pp. 1-10. [See also follow-up comments and counter-comments by John R. Suler, by Michael A. West, by Deane H. Shapiro, Jr., by Holmes, by Herbert Benson and Richard Friedman, and another by Holmes, in *American Psychologist,* 1985, 40(6), pp. 717-731.]

JUNG, C. G. *Modern Man in Search of a Soul.* New York:

Harcourt, Brace, 1933.

JUNG, C. G. *The Collected Works of C. G. Jung. Vol. 11: Psychology and Religion: West and East.* Princeton, NJ: Princeton University Press, 1958.

JUNG, C. G. *The Collected Works of C. G. Jung. Vol. 9: The Archetypes and the Collective Unconscious.* Princeton, NJ: Princeton University Press, 1959.

JUNG, C. G. "Commentary," in Richard Wilhelm (Trans.), *The Secret of the Golden Flower.* New York: Harcourt Brace Jovanovich, 1962, pp. 79-137.

KABAT-ZINN, JON. "An Outpatient Program in Behavioral Medicine for Chronic Pain Patients Based on the Practice of Mindfulness Meditation," *General Hospital Psychiatry,* 1982, 4, pp. 33-47.

KINDLER, HERBERT. "The Influence of a Meditation-Relaxation Technique on Group Problem-Solving Effectiveness," *Journal of Applied Behavioral Science,* 1979, 13(3). (Reported in *Perspective on Consciousness and Psi Research,* 1980, 2(1), p. 2.)

KOHR, RICHARD L. "An A.R.E. Survey of Meditation," *The A.R.E. Journal,* 1976, 11(4), pp. 174-182.

NARANJO, CLAUDIO, and ROBERT ORNSTEIN. *On the Psychology of Meditation.* New York: Viking Press, 1971.

OSIS, K. "ESP and Changed States of Consciousness Induced By Meditation," *Journal of the American Society for Psychical Research,* 1971, 65(1), pp. 17-65.

OTTO, R. *Mysticism East and West.* New York: Macmillan, 1932.

Perspective on Consciousness and Psi Research, a monthly research service published by the Association for Research and Enlightenment, Inc., Virginia Beach, VA.

PETERSON, DONALD. "Headache: Modern Concepts of

Diagnosis and Management," *Primary Care*, 1984 (December). (Reported in "Psi Research" in *Venture Inward*, 1985, 1(7), pp. 37-38.)

PURYEAR, HERBERT B., CHARLES THOMAS CAYCE, and MARK A. THURSTON. "Anxiety Reduction Associated with Meditation Home Study." *Perceptual and Motor Skills*, 1976, 43, pp. 527-531.

PURYEAR, HERBERT B., and MARK A. THURSTON. *Meditation and the Mind of Man.* Virginia Beach, VA: A.R.E. Press, 1978.

ROUSSELLE, ERWIN. "Spiritual Guidance in Contemporary Taosim," in J. Campbell (Ed.), *Papers from the Eranos Yearbooks. Vol. 4: Spiritual Disciplines.* Princeton, NJ: Princeton University Press, 1960, pp. 59-101.

SCHMECK, HAROLD M., JR. "As Scoffing Fades, Pineal Gland Gets Its Due," *New York Times*, January 31, 1984, p. C1.

SCHMEIDLER, G. R. "High ESP Scores After a Swami's Brief Instruction in Meditation and Breathing," *Journal of the American Society for Psychical Research*, 1970, 64(1), pp. 100-103.

SHAPIRO, DEANE H., JR. "Overview: Clinical and Physiological Comparison of Meditation with Other Self-Control Strategies," *American Journal of Psychiatry*, 1982, 139(3), pp. 267-274.

SPARROW, G. SCOTT. "A.R.E. Research Project: An Initial Analysis," *The A.R.E. Journal*, 1981, 16(3), pp. 101-112.

STANFORD, RAY. "Creation" (1976 revision), in Ray Stanford, *The Spirit Unto the Churches.* Austin, TX: Association for the Understanding of Man, 1977, pp. 191-210.

STANFORD, RAY. *The Spirit Unto the Churches* (1977 revision). Austin, TX: Association for the Understanding of Man, 1977.

THROLL, D. A. "Transcendental Meditation and Progressive Relaxation: Their Psychological Effects," *Journal of Clinical Psychology*, 1981, 37(4), pp. 776-781.

TRAVIS, FREDERICK. *Journal of Creative Behavior*, 13(3). (Article about meditation and creativity, reported in *Perspective on Consciousness and Psi Research*, 1980, 2(2), pp. 1-2.)

UNDERHILL, EVELYN. *Mysticism: A Study in the Nature and Development of Man's Spiritual Consciousness*. New York: Dutton, 1910.

Venture Inward, a bimonthly magazine published by the Association for Research and Enlightenment, Inc., Virginia Beach, VA.

WALLACE, ROBERT KEITH and HERBERT BENSON. "The Physiology of Meditation," in Robert Ornstein (Ed.), *The Nature of Human Consciousness*. New York: Viking Press, 1973.

WALLACE, ROBERT KEITH; MICHAEL DILLBECK; ELIHA JACOBE; and BETH HARRINGTON. "The Effects of the Transcendental Meditation and TM-Sidhi Program on the Aging Process," *International Journal of Neuroscience*, 1982, 16, pp. 53-58.

WARSHAL, DEBRA. "Effects of the Transcendental Meditation Technique on Normal and Jendrassik Reflex Time," *Perceptual and Motor Skills*, 1980, 50, pp. 1103-1106.

WEST, MICHAEL. "The Psychosomatics of Meditation," *Journal of Psychosomatic Research*, 1980, 24. (Reported in *Perspective on Consciousness and Psi Research*, 1981, 12(2), pp. 1, 4.)

WILHELM, RICHARD (Trans.). *The Secret of the Golden*

Flower. New York: Harcourt Brace Jovanovich, 1962.

WONG, MARTIN R.; NANCYE B. BROCHIN; and KAY L. GEN-
DRON. "Effects of Meditation on Anxiety and Chemical
Dependency," *Journal of Drug Education,* 1981, 11(2),
pp. 91-105.

STAY IN TOUCH
AND INFORMED

If you would like to receive periodic updates on the latest books and tapes from Inner Vision Publishing Co., send your name and address to:

Inner Vision
Box 1117, Seapines Station
Virginia Beach, VA 23451

Or Call Toll-Free:

1-800-227-0172
in Virginia call, 1-804-671-1777